Edizioni R.E.I.

All of our ebooks can be read out on the following devices: computer, eReader, IOS, Android, blackberry, windows, tablets, mobile phones.

Mantelli - Brown - Kittel - Graf

Wunderwaffen

The secret weapons of World War II

ISBN 978-2-37297-3267

Publishing and Printing: February 28, 2017
Edizioni R.E.I.
www.edizionirei.webnode.com
edizionirei@outlook.com

Mantelli - Brown - Kittel - Graf

Wunderwaffen

The secret weapons
of World War II

Edizioni R.E.I.

Index

Wunderwaffen - The secret weapons

Vergeltungswaffen, retaliatory weapon, was a term coined during the Second World War to represent some Wunderwaffe, miraculous weapons, that Germany was developing. The "miracle" weapons, according to the propaganda, would have given a clear technological superiority of the German army and would have radically changed the course of the conflict, which has now clearly turned in favor of the Allies. The most famous Wunderwaffe, as well as some of the few to have been completed and widely used, were the Vergeltungswaffe, "vengeance weapons"; most still Wunderwaffe remained at the project level, as the German military nuclear program, or prototypes, such as the Panzer VIII Maus.

Among the most famous are cited: the V1 flying bomb, rocket V2 and V3 cannon. While the V1 can be considered a first draft of cruise missile, as it was flying on a cruise route to the target before you fall on the objective, the V2 rocket was the first real man-made and used in an armed conflict. Initially these weapons had their own names, but for the purposes of propaganda, Joseph Goebbels coined the name Vergeltungswaffen, "retaliatory weapon" because it was the British first to bomb the popular districts of German cities, slaughtering innocent civilians.

The V-1

The Fieseler Fi 103, better known as the V-1, designated internally as in FZG Code 76 (Flakzielgerät - target for anti-aircraft artillery), was a military weapon developed by the German Fieseler in the early forties and used by the Luftwaffe in the last phase of World war II. The V-1, the abbreviation stands for Vergeltungswaffen 1, translated from the German reprisal Weapon 1 and so renamed by Joseph Goebbels for propaganda purposes, combined the characteristics of a plane to those of an aviation bomb and can be considered the first example of cruise missile.

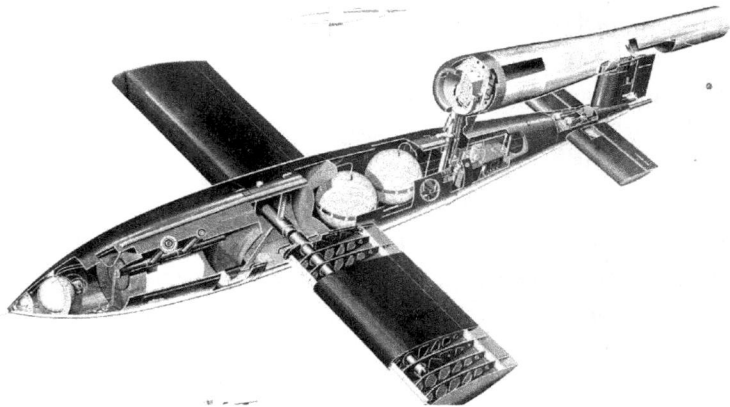

In autumn 1936, while working for the company aircraft engine Argus, fritz gosslau, on the experience gained on the Argus As 292 (military designation FZG 43), a small reconnaissance aircraft controlled remotely, began working on the development of the system of the remote control aircraft. On 9 November 1939, the company sent to Reichsluftfahrtministerium, the ministry at the time responsible for civil aviation and military of Germany, a preliminary project for the construction of a remote-controlled aircraft.

On a private initiative, the Argus, asking collaboration in the Lorentz and Arado Flugzeugwerke, he started a development first as Project "Fernfeuer". The aircraft, called simply lufttorpedo, torpedo steering wheel, was proposed in three variants capable of carrying a 1,000 kg payload to an operational altitude of 5,000 meters, which included the first was equipped with a 12-cylinder V reversed Argus As 410 from PS 500, at a cruising speed of 700 km / h, the last with a new type of engine then to the early stages of development, the Pulsejet, a jet engine able to provide 150 kg of thrust and which would have guaranteed the object a cruise speed provided for 750 km / h. A further development, which took over the internal Project P 35 "Erfurt designation", was again presented to the RLM Gosslau authorities in April 1940, but the following 31 May Rudolf Bree replied that he saw possible uses of such a solution, and that the remote control of the bomb project was further weakness.

On January 6, 1941 Heinrich Koppenberg, the director of Argus, in an attempt to save the project obtained a meeting with Ernst Udet to try to convince him to continue its development but Udet he announced his decision to cancel it. Nonetheless Gosslau was convinced that the basic idea was solid again and began working to simplify the project. Since the Argus, being an engine manufacturer, lacked the ability to produce a fuselage for the project, Koppenberg asked Robert Lusser, chief designer and head of the technical office Heinkel, to be able to assist in the development stages. The February 27, 1942 Lusser, which since January 22 he had moved to Fieseler, was able to meet with Koppenberg and to capture the details of the Gosslau project. Lusser will further modified configuration abandoning the proposed solution with two pulsogetto engines for a single engine. The final development of the project was presented to the Technical Office RLM June 5 next obtaining the approval, the official designation to

Fieseler Fi 103 and assigning the task to furnish the prototype for the feedback. On 19 June, the Generalfeldmarschall Erhard Milch gave Fi 103 the highest priority to start it as soon as possible to mass production and the development program was transferred to the testing center of the Luftwaffe in Karlshagen. The V-1 was developed in the secret base of Peenemunde, located about 230 km from Berlin, on the banks of the Baltic Sea. This gigantic center, built in 1937, included a large number of laboratories and a huge manufacturing center; next, a city was built for engineers, staff and their families. This center, under the direction of Walter Dornberger and Wernher Von Braun, employing more than 12,000 people and was the most modern in the world at the beginning of World War II. On August 30, the Fiesler completed the first cell and the first prototype flew Fi 103 December 10, 1942, when it was dropped from a Focke-Wulf Fw 200 specially equipped for gliding flight. The V-1 were designed to be less expensive and simple as possible; each had a cost of 3,500 Marks, which corresponded to 1/10 of the price of a V-2 rocket. The first flight was conducted December 23, 1942 with the launch carried out by a ramp; the prototype covers a distance of only 3 Km. Many developments were made and you can tell that the device was finally in place 26 June 1943 with the launch of the prototype number 65 who traveled a distance of 234 Km.

Technology

The V-1 was designed as in Kirschkern (cherry pit code) to be Lusser and Gosslau, with a fuselage constructed mainly of welded steel plates and wings made with the same technique, or plywood. The simple Pulsejet worked with about 50 pulses per second and the characteristic hum product procured to bomb the buzz nickname. The flying bomb used a motor to Pulsejet Argus As 014. This type of aircraft engine could not be validly employed for air driven by war, as difficult to start, inefficient above 3,000 meters, of poor durability and practically not able to change speed. All these characteristics were rather widely compatible with a flying bomb, which could instead take advantage of the great constructive simplicity of this type of engines, joined in of absolute importance of speed performance for the time. Great features vibrations produced by Pulse jet, led to the installation outside and rear Argus. It was produced around 31,100 specimens.

It provided a thrust of 272 kg corresponding to approximately 700 hp at cruising speed. In the first model, tried November 13, 1939, the air entered in the engine at the rear, was accelerated by a device called Borda mouth which also conducted compression and recirculation of the mixture of air and fuel in the combustion chamber to then be ejected from the nozzle exhaust, constituted by a conduit coaxial to the input. This configuration was quickly discarded because of the uneven combustion.

The second model provided for the front air inlet pressure in a spherical combustion chamber where it was deflected, giving rise to an annular vortex. From the third model then it was eliminated in the mouth of Borda, and the resulting vortex ring, by applying an input to reed valve developed by the German scientist Paul Schmidt. The first engine was test flown April 28, 1941, installed on a biplane Gotha Go

145 specially modified. In the summer of 1942, a pair of engines was installed on a transport glider DFS 230-A1, which, after being driven at high altitude and dropped, it turned and became the first aircraft in the world to fly pushed by pulsogetti, although procured engines other damage to the structure of the glider. It was also tested on the Messerschmitt Bf 110 to try to increase the maximum speed, but experiments on the aircraft were soon set aside to focus efforts on the V-1 flying bombs. In August 1944 the last change to the fuel control system was made which enabled him to reach the V- speed of 765 km / h. In its final version, the engine was constituted by a metal sheet folded to form a tube; They were placed in front of a series of reed valves controlled by springs, a fuel injection system and a spark plug. To start the engine was placed a nozzle cap to saturate the combustion chamber with acetylene; simultaneously the spark of the spark plug, a portable source of compressed air provided the oxygen needed for start for the time necessary to the stabilization of the operating temperature. At that point it was removed the electrical and pneumatic power and the burning continued self-subsisting. Each cycle, or pulse, the motor started with open valves. The downstream injected fuel was ignited and the consequent expansion of the combustion gases carrying the closure valves, but the subsequent drop in pressure in the combustion chamber due to the expulsion of the exhaust gases from the nozzle reopened valves, new air flowed and so the cycle could be repeated at a frequency of about 45-55 times per second. The electric ignition system was used only at start; to scheme was the flashback into the nozzle to ensure the ignition of the fresh mixture. The fuel tank, typically petrol, was put into the compressed air pressure also used by the automatic guidance system. The fuel control system provided, in a continuous manner, the fuel to the injectors at a variable pressure depending on the flight condition.

Pulse jet Argus As 014 installed on a cross-section of V-1.

Unlike other Pulse jet era, who used a shut-off valve of the air intake structured like the petals of a flower, the Argus used for the V-1 was using a metal grid created with spacers. Along the openings of the grid of small rectangular lamellas they were mounted, riveted on one side and free to vibrate on the other, so as to close or open the passages for the incoming air, depending on the pressure that prevails inside, due the explosion in the combustion chamber, or the aerodynamic pressure produced by the air. In the V-1, the cycle is repeated 47 times per second. This system of metal plates was simple to build, and did not require skilled labor or sophisticated equipment, valuable characteristics in wartime. To 76 cm behind the grill of the air intake was placed the combustion chamber, in which the first power was commanded by a car-based candle, powered by independent electric unit then disconnected at launch. The fuel, the common, low-octane gasoline, was injected directly by exploiting the pressure of the compressed air supply also used to keep rotating the gyroscopes to guide and to move the control surfaces.

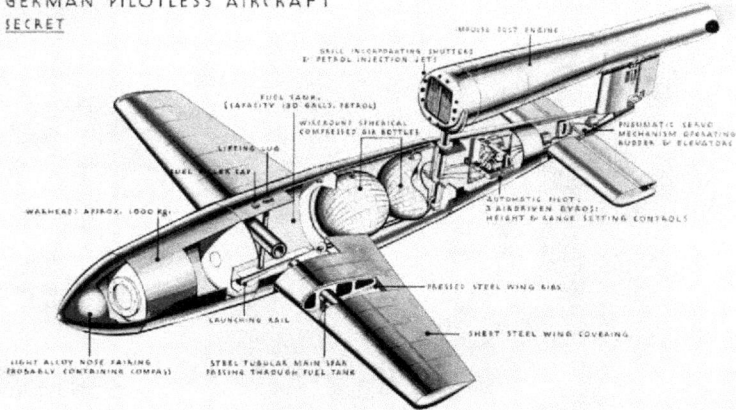

Three nozzles for the air in front of the jet pulse were connected to an external source of compressed air, which was used for starting the engine. For the ignition was usually used Acetylene gas, and very often a panel of wood (or similar) was placed at the end of the exhaust pipe to prevent release of fuel before ignition. Once the engine was started and the temperature had reached the minimum operating level, the external air hose and connectors were removed, and the engine started to "shoot" pulses without the need for additional electrical ignition systems: these, in fact , it was only required to allow the engine to start. According to a widespread myth, the engine Argus As 014 of the V-1 required a minimum speed of 240 km / h to work. In fact, this pulse jet was able to operate also at a fixed point: it was possible thanks to the intake valves synchronized with the ignition of the mixture in the combustion chamber.

Archive footage of that period clearly show the characteristic discharge of the engine at full throttle button, depending on the weapon before the departure from the launch catapult.

The origin of this myth is probably due to the fact that, since the static thrust of the pulse jet rather low and the stall speed of the small very high wings, the V-1 would not have been able to take off from one of short distances, and which therefore call for an aircraft catapult or an airborne drop by a modified bomber, like a Heinkel He 111. The terrestrial launch of the V-1, usually, occurred thanks to a launch ramp inclined by an apparatus known as Dampferzeuger ("steam") generator which used hydrogen peroxide and potassium permanganate (T-Stoff and Z-Stoff). The take-off took place at the speed of 580 km / h.

As of January 1941, the pulse jet of V-1 was tested on a wide variety of vehicles, including cars and a boat from experimental attack known as the Tornado. This vessel, which was unsuccessful, was a variant of a Sprengboot: according to the designers, this vessel, laden with explosives, would have to be guided towards a target ship as a pilot, he would have to leave the boat at the last minute. The Tornado was assembled using the seaplane hulls connected in catamaran, with a small cockpit on connecting beams. The Tornado prototype was judged by the noisy and disappointing performance, and was then abandoned in favor of more conventional boats, propelled by normal piston engines. The engine, however, operated its first flight April 30, 1941, mounted on a Gotha Go 145.

The Pulsejet

The Pulsejet, or pulse-jet, is a very simple form of jet engine in which combustion occurs intermittently providing a boost pulse. Unlike the ramjet (the jet engine which most resembles), is able to provide a boost to fixed point (ie at flight speeds nothing). The first studies on the pulse jet date back to the early twentieth century, when in France Victor De Karavodine patented, April 10, 1907, the first Pulsejet model. In 1910 he was awarded a patent also the engineer Belgian Georges Marconnet, but both solutions were at the stage of laboratory models. With the end of World War also the military interest in this type of engine went dying. In 1939 the Reich Air Ministry decided to promote the search engine jet and assigned to each engine house a different technological solution to develop. At Argus touched pulsogetto that with As 014 model designed by German engineer fritz gosslau, find its first practical application of the V-1. Later were used, but always remain in the field of experimentation, some Pulse jet mounted on helicopters. In this case the engines were placed at the ends of the rotor blades. Mounted according to this scheme the Pulse jet showed the great advantage of not producing the characteristic torque, thus allowing to create simpler aircraft without a tail rotor and the related transmission systems. The Pulse jet are characterized by an extreme simplicity and by a low production cost.
The main flaw is their high noise and from fuel consumption, which limits their scope to military posts and a few other applications. Today, the increased use of pulse jet occurs in the dynamic model aircraft.
As many jet engines the Pulsejet is an engine very simple design internal combustion, consisting in practice in a long tube inside which the air enters, is mixed with fuel to create a fuel mixture. The difference that distinguishes

from others Pulse jet engines, such as turbo-jet or ramjet, is constituted by the fact that the combustion that takes place inside the engine is not a continuous process but is in the form of repeated explosions, pulses, from which also derives the same engine name.

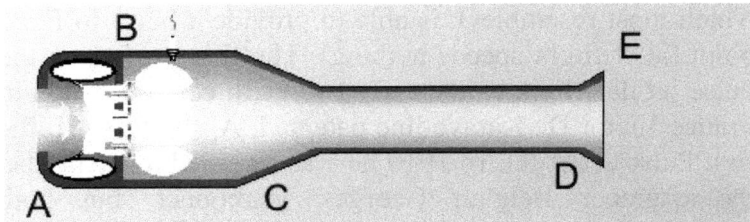

A) intake and fuel injection
B) valves
C) of the combustion chamber
D) nozzle
E) expelled gases.

In practice the Pulsejet works with the outside air inlet from the front, where it is located or not the valve, this is mixed with the fuel that is injected into the combustion chamber. Here the mixture is ignited and finally the flue gases exit from the back thus producing the thrust.
The first ignition must be carried out by entering compressed air with a compressor or an air cylinder, the engine or simply forcing it in via the air intake.

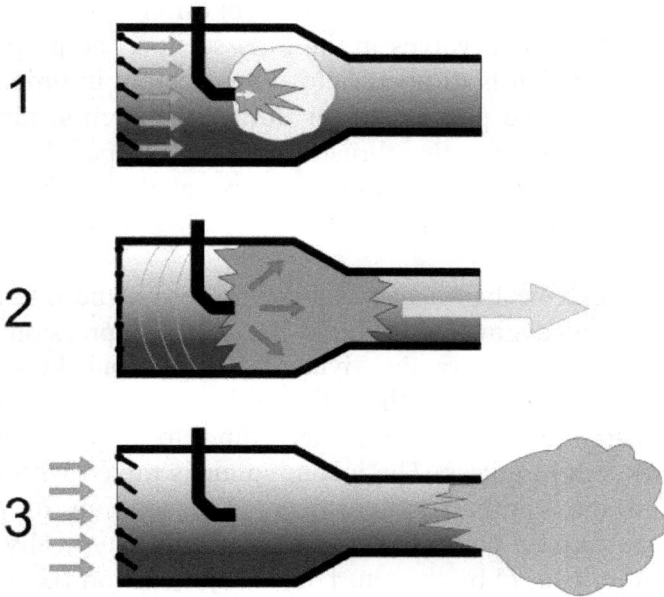

Diagram of the valve Pulsejet:

- In the first image the injected fuel is mixed with the incoming air from the left end and, via an appropriate initial power system (during normal operation it is usually possible to exploit the backfire for the ignition) triggers the combustion of the mixture created.

- In the figure number two the developed combustion generates pressure waves that propagate throughout the system, and consequently the expansion due to combustion has the leak of gas from the right end, that expulsion creates a vacuum in the inlet section of the system that allows to suck the air for the next cycle (figure three).

- In the figure are also visible (in different positions) of the reed valves in the inlet section, the purpose of which is to open / close this section in order to allow the passage of air during the suction phase and prevent the thrust that is developed by the expulsion of the gases is propagated also through the suction section.

The Pulsejet is then a very simple to design the internal combustion engine, in which the air compression is captured, as for the ramjet, dynamically, without the need of a compressor; unlike the other esoreattori the combustion does not occur according to a continuous process, but in pulses. The incoming air is mixed with the fuel in the combustion chamber. The ignition of the mixture can be controlled by a glow plug (typically at startup) or caused by the return of the combustion flame of the previous step (a scheme).

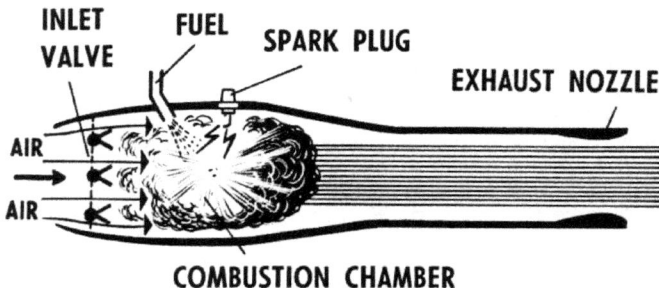

The resulting increase in pressure causes the acceleration and the expulsion of the burnt gas exhaust from the nozzle, thus providing the thrust. Backflow through the air inlet is prevented by mechanical valves or "aerodynamic" (in valveless engines). The next depression that is to have in the combustion chamber draws new air and the cycle can thus be repeated between 40 and 250 times per second, depending on the type and size of the engine. One of the particularities of the Pulsejet is that of being able to self-feed, or of spontaneously suck the comburent air thanks to the depression that is to be generated in the front section of the device, a feature that makes the Pulsejet capable of providing also pushing the fixed point (zero speed), once ignited.

Basically there are two types of Pulsejet:

- Pulse jet valves
  In this configuration the flow of gas inside the engine is partly controlled by a system of valves that edge, acting as a check valve, allows the passage of gases in one direction only.

Reed valve.

The Achilles heel of this solution is given by the fragility of the slats which limits the operational life of the engine to a few hours of continuous operation.

- Pulse jet without valves

The first pulse jet models were constructed without valves (valveless), but using particular geometric configurations (such as, for example, the Borda mouth) is trying to create swirling flows with the dual purpose to mix the incoming air with the fuel and increase the pressure of the confining mixture in the combustion chamber. These first configurations, however, were particularly inefficient because of the fresh mixture losses ejected from the air intake and the total pressure losses due to the induced turbulence.

In the late forties and mid-fifties he tried to investigate "aerodynamic valves" that "tuning" the geometry of the air intake nozzle and with the resonance of pressure waves allow a smooth operation and efficiencies of to those of engines with reed valves. Among these engines "Escopette" and "Ecrevisse" of the French SNECMA or AS-11 installed on the Dutch drone Aviolanda AT-21. The total lack of furniture in these configuration parts allow advantages in terms of reliability and low construction costs. A development of Pulsejet, which is still carried out, is the Pulse Detonation Engine or PDE. This motor has a very similar operation to a traditional Pulsejet but generates its propulsive force across the detonation and not the deflagration of the fuel / air mixture. This new type of engine promises efficiencies comparable (if not superior) to the turbofan, especially at high flight speeds.
The first flight of an aircraft powered by a Pulse Detonation Engine took place at the Mojave Air and Space Port January 31, 2008. The main difference between a PDE and a traditional pulsogetto is that the mixture in the combustion chamber does not effect a subsonic combustion, but is brought to fulfill a supersonic detonation. In PDE, the oxygen and fuel combine generating gas that move at supersonic speeds (in practice

it is an explosion rather than a combustion). The other difference, is that the closing valves are replaced by more sophisticated devices, although in some projects of PDE of General Electric, is eliminated each closing device thanks to a careful choice of the times, using the pressure differences between the different areas of the engine, in order to ensure that the hot gases are expelled backwards.

Technical specifications

- Length: 3,66 meters
- Diameter: 588 mm
- exhaust pipe diameter: 380 mm
- Tailpipe Length: 1,75metri
- Weight: 153 kg
- Static Thrust: 500 pounds
- Maximum load: 800 pounds
- Fuel consumption: 3,4kg / lb / hr

Analysis of the thermodynamic cycle

The operation of the pulse jet is based fundamentally on the Effect venturi, more precisely in conjunction with the lower section of the combustion chamber area. The described thermal cycle is said to Lenoir and is characterized by the total absence of the compression process, which results in a much lower thermodynamic efficiency compared to the classic Otto and Diesel cycles.

Step combustion (1-2)
Point 1 represents the initial condition of the fluid (air-fuel mixture) that fills the combustion chamber. The introduction of heat q1 referred to the unit of mass, it produces a constant volume combustion. In this phase, the work is zero.

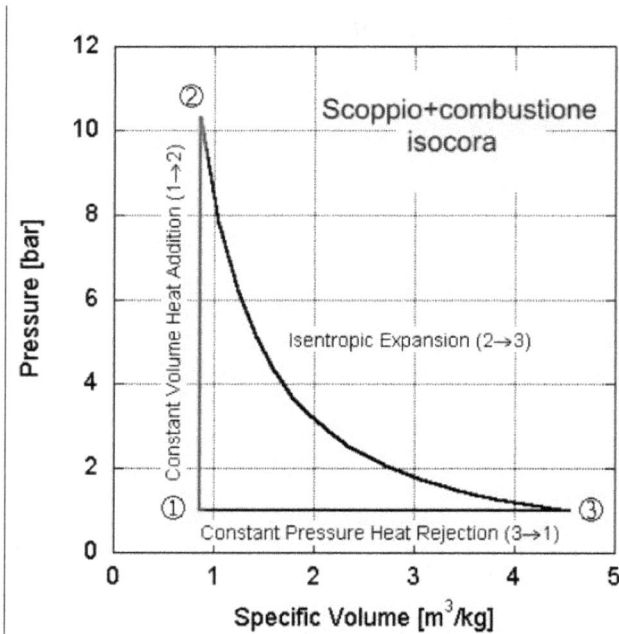

Expansion phase (2-3)

The expansion takes place in a reversible adiabatic and returns the fluid at the original pressure. This is the only active phase of the cycle.

The work is given by the equation: L3 = m * hp (T2 - T3).

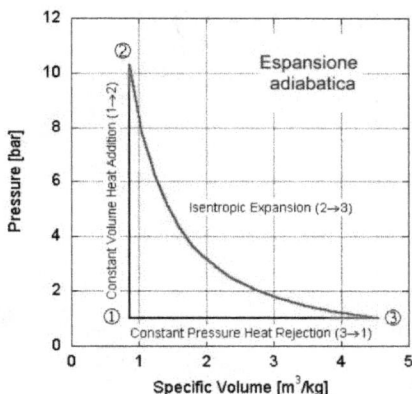

Discharge phase (3-1)

During the discharge phase, the fluid is returned to the original temperature by means of a constant-pressure cooling. In this phase, the work is given by the relation: L4 = p1 * (V1-V3).

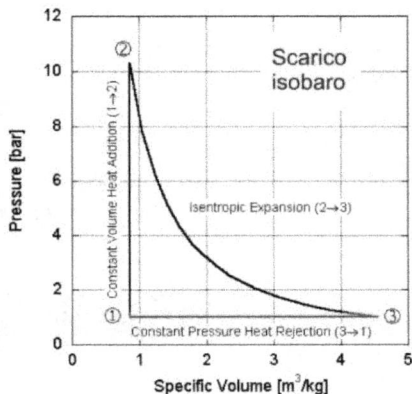

The useful work is represented graphically by the enclosed by the p-V graphic and true: Ltot = L3 + L4.
The yield on the other hand is calculated by dividing the total work and the heat Q2 necessary to initiate combustion and is given by:

$$\eta_{tot} = L_{tot} \, / \, m{*}c_v * (T_2 - T_1)$$

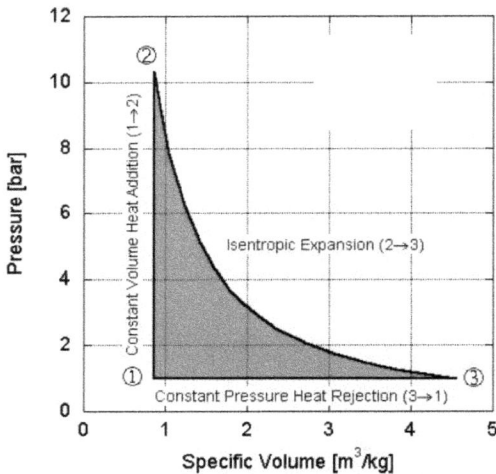

Constant Volume Heat Addition (1→2)

Isentropic Expansion (2→3)

Constant Pressure Heat Rejection (3→1)

Pressure [bar]

Specific Volume [m³/kg]

Guide system

The guidance system of the V-1 was constituted by a simple automatic pilot able to adjust altitude and speed, developed by Askania of Berlin.

A pendulum system that oscillated back and forth along the longitudinal axis of the aircraft was adjusted and stabilized by a gyro and provided the data for the measure and the buoyancy control on the axis of pitching. The energy required to power both the device of the gyroscope is the actuators for flight controls was provided by two large spherical tanks loaded before launch with compressed air to 150 atmospheres (15,000 kPa), who also had the task of pressurizing the reservoir fuel. Gyro was initialized to the ground before the launch and was the component dedicated to providing the feedback of the attitude control system. To control the yaw over the pitch and roll, his gyroscope was tilted out of the horizontal plane defined by the longitudinal and roll attitude axes so as to react to changes of trim on the three degrees of freedom. The gyroscope was kept aligned by a magnetic compass and the bow and stern pendulums. This interaction meant that it was sufficient to change the direction of the use of the rudder without the use of ailerons. In a V-1 landed without exploding in March 1945 in the Netherlands, between Tilburg and Goirle, were found about six rolls of the Nazi propaganda magazine "Signal" inserted in the wing spar steel tube left, used to balance statically l ' bomb before launch. It is also known that many V-1 before launch were equipped with a small radio transmitter (consisting of a triode marked 'S3', but equivalent in a moment to the power tube type RL2.4T1), to control the direction flight between the launch point and the coordinates of the target with respect to a radio bow. An odometer actuated by a vane anemometer positioned on the front of the aircraft when it was determined the goal was reached, with sufficient accuracy to the bombing. Prior to the launch, a counter was set to a value that reached zero at the time of arrival at destination in windy conditions estimated. After takeoff, the airflow azionava propeller and every 30 spins the propeller advancing device unit and provided to arm the warhead after about 60 km. When the counter immunity timer were detonated two explosive bolts. The two flaps of the BCs were operated, the connection between the balancer and actuator was blocked and a guillotine device cut the hoses to the rudder servo control leaving him free. These operations were tasked to put the V-1 dive. Originally the dive was designed to be conducted with the engine at full power but in practice the maneuver caused the interruption of the flow of fuel and the consequent stopping of the motor. The sudden silence after the classic ringing warned the people in the impending impact. The fuel problem was later resolved and the latest operating specimens reached the goal at full speed. Thanks to the counter, which determined the flight distance, the V-1 could be launched with the ramp bet approximately in the desired direction and the autopilot would have been able to control the flight. The pulse jet engine Argus could not produce the necessary thrust for takeoff, and then the V-1 was dropped using a ramp of 48 meters equipped with a steam catapult system, designed by Walter society. The ramp contained a slot fitted with a handlebar piston, with the flying bomb placed on a simple trailer connected to the piston. The piston was held in place with a safety pin. The cart was made up of a reaction chamber with water tanks peroxide (HO) and granules of potassium permanganate (KMnO4) as catalyst, and was connected to a chamber at the base of the ramp whose other end was connected to the piston. When the hydrogen peroxide was pumped in potassium permanganate, it is converted in large quantities of hot steam that accumulated in the pressure against the piston.

The front with the vanes anemometer, the release lever and the selectors 4 for adjustments before departure.

When the pressure reached a certain level, the piston of the safety pin broke and the carriage was rapidly moved up the ramp. The V-1 thus left the launching ramp at a speed of about 400 km / h.

Use

The first complete cell of a V-1 was delivered on August 30, 1942. After that it was available the first engine, in September, was made the first test flight, October 28, 1942, at Peenemunde. The V-1 flew docked under a Focke-Wulf Fw 200. For the first flight test with engine running, however, must wait until December 10, when a specimen was dropped from a He-111 bomber, transporting him hooked in the lower. A legend relates that the Stabilisation and driving problems were solved thanks to a daring test flight from the famous aviatrix Hanna Reitsch, who would put it personally driving a V-1 specially modified to carry human spaceflight. The conventional launch sites could theoretically launch about fifteen V-1 a day. This, however, was a pace that was hard to keep, at least on a consistent basis. However, the maximum reached was eighteen. Overall, only 15% of the bombs hit their target, while the majority was lost because of the prepared counter-measures by the Allies, mechanical problems or driving errors. The operating portion, initially, was expected to be around 2,750 meters. However, because of repeated failures of the fuel barometric pressure regulator, the Germans were forced to lower this share in May 1944, which would, in fact, the V-1 in range of 40 mm Bofors guns, widely used by allied anti-aircraft units.

The trial versions of the V-1 were aviolanciate.

In the operating environment, most of the bombs was launched from fixed land installations (step Calais and Dutch coasts), although between July 1944 and January 1945, the Luftwaffe launched it approximately 1,176 specimens from modified Heinkel He 111 bombers, belonging Kampfgeschwader 3 to that operated on the North Sea.

Besides the obvious reason to continue the bombing campaign even after the loss of terrestrial installations on the French coast, the air landing supplied the Luftwaffe the opportunity to circumvent the increasingly effective countermeasures put in place by the Allies to counteract this type of weapons, as well as to increase the range.

To minimize the risks associated with these operations (especially that of being detected by radar), the German crews developed a tactic called "lo-hi-lo": the He-111 should have, after leaving their air bases and passed the coast, down to a slight increase in flight. After coming close to the launch point, the crews were to take off again, throwing the bomb, and declined rapidly previous to the altitude, so you come back. Searches after the war showed that the failure rate was 40%, and the He-111 used for this purpose were extremely vulnerable to night fighters: this was due to the fact that the brightness produced by the departure of the V1 illuminating the area around all 'air carrier for a few seconds. During the war, they were produced over 30,000 specimens. Each of these required 350 hours of work (including 120 for the autopilot), at a cost that was 4% of that of a V-2, with a comparable weapons load (830 kg charge at high Amatol potential, ie trinitrotoluene and ammonium nitrate, but sometimes they used a type of explosive economic, the Danarit). The first flying bomb fell on Swanscombe, near Gravesend, situated on the Thames east of London, on June 13, 1944 at 4:18 pm; this first bomb falls into a field and causes a crater about five meters in diameter by almost a meter (0.90 cm). Although he not seriously damaged a house victims. That same night were launched only a dozen V-1, contrary to what he had expected the German general who was involved:

- Two hours before dawn, throwing 300 V-1.
- At noon, launch of 100 V-1 and in the afternoon 2-3 launches per hour.
- In the evening, a large launch of V-1 as curfews.

In the first 10 days, 370 V-1 struck London.
Soon the answer was organized and the fighters went to intercept the flying bombs on the English Channel, as well as the response of anti-aircraft and the installation of barrage balloons in the outskirts of London. These measures began to bear fruit, as in a day, about 97 V-1 launched by the Germans, only four hit London. It was also asked the British to not point out in the obituaries of newspapers the nature of death, to avoid giving information to the Germans that they had no precise information about the place of the crash of the flying bombs. In addition, the counter espionage began broadcasting false information about the fall of the V-1, indicating the exact number of bombs dropped too far from the original target, while for those arriving on the lens were communicated false information corresponding to places far from the center of the city. Overall, Britain

was joined by about 10,000 weapons of this type: the London, particularly the capital, it was hit 3,564 times, with the killing of 6,184 people and injuring 17,981 more. The highest density of V-1 fell from Croydon, south-east of the city. Other 1,600 were pulled from the He-111H-22. Missiles, 1,847 were pulled down by fighters like the P-51, the Spitfire and others, 10-12 from naval guns, 232 from the brake cables of the balloons, 1878 by flak. 31,600 homes were destroyed and more than a million damaged ones. British casualties caused by German bombers had been around 51,509, but now the Germans could no longer afford to bombing campaigns with conventional aircraft.

But the British had not only been victims and damage to civilians: it seems that the affected factories, considering only those with strategic interests, had been as many as 50 in the capital, and 919 in other regions, which required 6.5 million man-hours and 21,000 people, with a fall in production of 10% of British industry. If the official figures speak of 275,000 people dislodged from London, actually known data from 1994 say 1,450,000, so the workforce was reduced by much. The loss for the Air Ministry was specified in 47.6 million pounds, more than 450 aircraft and 2,900 men lost for law enforcement actions to these weapons (perhaps including strike actions on the ground on the ramps). An extensive bombing of Peenemunde operation was launched by the RAF on the night between 17 and 18 August 1943 (Operation Hydra) with the use of 597 bombers (Lancaster 324, 219 Halifax and Stirling 54), of which 94 were Pathfinder (special units to report with bright bombs goals) that were supposed to hit, in sequence, the residences of the scientists, two large factories, design workshops and administrative offices. At the head of this he was put the pilot John Searby. This raid killed about 700 people, including Walter Thiel, head of engine development. This

33

raid prompted him to move production of the V rockets underground. Despite the raids, many installations of Peenemünde remained intact at the end of World War II, as most of the bombs were dropped on residential areas and on foreign workers camps. There are many disputes about how the Allies discovered the existence of Peenemunde. The British official version states that all the information was collected thanks to aerial reconnaissance. However, testimonies and documents claim that the Polish underground army intelligence (Home Army or AK), and information from other sources (including a Danish pilot who photographed what looked like a rocket V) unveiled Peenemunde. The British intelligence for years denied having received any information about Peenemünde from Poland. At any copies of reports they emerged in Poland after the war. R. V. Jones contradicted himself: first denied the fact, later in his book The Wizard War wrote that many bombs fell on the fields of foreign workers who gave information to the Allies; He said that these Polish workers belonged to AK. In recent years, politicians and Polish historians have requested access to British archives (since the United Kingdom has many, if not all, of the AK relationships). Currently the UK authorities responded that all of the AK reports were destroyed. On July 18, 1944 and August 4 was the turn of 413 Boeing B-17 "Flying Fortresses". The research center suffered heavy damage from the 1,600 tons of bombs dropped, however, some important buildings were saved, as well as its archives, allowing you to continue the operation, after having provided to camouflage the plants. However, aware that these plants were no longer protected by the bombing, Hitler ordered to install under the mountains of the V1 production workshops, installing them near Nordhausen, in Mittelwerk, under the mountain of the Harz (code-named Dora) and use labor concentration camp, under the direction of German engineers, in order to avoid leaks. The subsoil was an old mine calcium carbonate (chalk), used since the 20's, and consists of two parallel tunnels 1,800 meters long and 46 transverse tunnels 150 meters (this was the distance of the two main galleries). The plan was to leave the two tunnels as service roads with railroads to the port and the withdrawal of the material, and do workshops in 46 galleries. They are made to get there (September 1943) 17.000 were deported from Buchenwald who else immediately to work (cleaning and concreting of tunnels). The rapidity of the decisions does take second place the housing problem of the deportees who, in six months, see the sun twice during the pest control: are infested with lice; not have water to drink, breathe ammonia vapors that burn the lungs, so much so that in six months 6,500 prisoners die. Finally, in February 1944, Albert Speer gets permission to visit the camp. It is said remains baffled by the situation; He makes it clear to the SS that is counterproductive teach the craft if after a few months you have to start over; order to be immediately built the external field; send material wagons, they do get other deportees from Buchenwald and in a month are being built 56 huts scattered in the field; everything is fenced by barbed wire with high voltage current. Finally the deportees, after 12 hours of work, they can get out of the tunnels, wash and sleep in the bunks. Mortality decreases, the output frequency of the missile becomes regular (500/550 per month), 2,000 of them in June and July 1944 are launched on London and 1000 in Antwerp.

The Allied air force course can not bomb the tunnels and then destroys bridges, railways, roads; razed the city of Nordhausen, where there are workshops of components for missiles; bombards a factory at Buchenwald, causing 364 deaths in the field. The output clock of missiles decreases until they ceased entirely. Then the SS begin to be walled up the entrances of tunnels, because none of the deportees missile builders must survive. But the population of

Nordhausen, terrified by the continuous bombardment, the strength of the lager inputs and takes refuge in the tunnels, destroying the project of SS. Then they began the so-called death marches, because none of the deportees must survive. Finally, April 14, 1945, the Americans arrive. The commander is accompanied by some survivors in all categories: discover a hundred missiles and tons of projects; He warns the command. You order to restore a railway line, it hunts the 500 technicians, including von Braun and the general, and the whole, in late June, is shipped to Antwerp and left for America. Via the Americans came the Russians. Also inspect their tunnels: uncover some missiles forgotten by Americans; but they are in possession of an unexpected gift unintentionally left by their predecessors: tons of construction projects, a boon for Russian designers. After which the inputs are undermined and destroyed and no longer know what it was; and the silence lasts for 53 years, because neither one nor the other had interest in getting to know that their space enterprises were the result of all that they had stolen in the Dora tunnels, despite the protests of the survivors who had urged their governments to did she light on that lager. Finally, in 1998, in the number 26 of the famous German magazine "Stern", appear dozens of color photographs of the Dora concentration camp, with prisoners to work in the tunnels. What had happened? The Nazis had photographers everywhere; Also in the Dora tunnels there was a photographer: he had taken dozens of slides, hidden in a pack in his suitcase. After the war, perhaps for some ill-concealed fear, he had returned home and hid the suitcase in the garage. In 1998, aged 91, was admitted to a senior institution. The son goes to sbaraccare his father's house and in the suitcase, in the garage, find your slides. At the end of the war, Von Braun was working on plans for a missile, the V-3, capable of hitting New York. Did not have time to realize it, he collapsed before the Third Reich. The young engineer could run the risk of being considered a war criminal and find himself in Nuremberg, although he had worked on the Army dependencies and not the SS. But he also knew that they would forgive the Americans as long as everything was over on their side. Thus in Reutte, a village of Tyrol, surrendered to US troops with a hundred employees and with the Peenemunde installations, promptly removed from the Soviets. He was received with full honors, and in 1950 was already an American citizen. Since September 1944, however, the threat of V1 for England was temporarily interrupted, due to the loss (capture or destruction) of the French coastal installations from which were made the launches. For this reason, then the V1 was used primarily to attack strategic targets in Belgium (especially the port of Antwerp): between October 1944 and March 1945, the country as a whole, was hit by 2448 bombs. The V-1 destroyed fighter, anti-aircraft guns and barrage balloons were 4,261. The last V-1 fell in England March 29, 1945, in Datchworth Hertfordshire: it was the last enemy action on English soil of World War II. The English defense against the German long-range weapons was called Operation Crossbow. Anti-aircraft guns were redeployed to different movements: first in mid-June 1944 by positions on the North Downs to the south coast, then along a drawstring Thames for attacks from the east.

In September 1944, a new line of defense was prepared on the East Anglian coast, and finally in December was adopted a new defensive configuration along the coast between Lincolnshire and Yorkshire. The implementations were influenced by the changes of approach lines of the V-1 launch sites having been reached by the advance of the Allies. The first night of sustained bombardment, the troops manning the anti-aircraft near Croydon exulted: unpredictably was shot down unprecedented numbers of

German bombers, most of the targets were reduced to flames or hit the engine, they rushed.

However, there was great disappointment when another truth became apparent. The anti-aircraft gunners soon found that these small and fast objectives were, in fact, extremely difficult to hit. The altitude of the V1 cruise, between 600 and 900 meters, was slightly higher than the effective range of light anti-aircraft guns and just below the optimum height of engagement of the heavy flak. Other countermeasures were the barrage balloons and the use of interceptors. Some RAF pilots, as Jean Maridor, used an original system to destroy the V1 without use of their hunting weapons. In fact, approaching the V-1, they positioned their wing under the wing of the bomb and progressively, acting with the ailerons, the destabilized by changing the trajectory to make it fall into the sea or however far from population centers. This method was developed by the officer pilot Johnny Faulkner, operating in 91 Squadron, the same Jean Maridor. Another method was to go at full speed close to V-1 that could be so unbalanced by the propeller turbulence. The planes used were the Supermarine Spitfire XIVdel 91 Squadron which destroyed 189 V1, the Hawker Typhon of 137 Squadron that shot down 30 flying bombs and Hawker Tempest of 602 Squadron commanded at the end of the war from Ace Aviation Pierre Clostermann that they destroyed 481 V-1.

Versions

The V-1 was built in different versions:

- FI 103 A1 - Standard version.

- FI 103 A2 - modified version of A1 with a Pulsejet which gave a speed of about 800 Km / h.

- FI 103 B1 - Built with a Pulsejet Porsche 109 005, with wooden spinner, tanks increased from 602 to 689 liters and increase the wing span to 5.74 m.

- FI 103 B2 - With explosive Trialen 105 or 106 'aluminized' to increase the power.

- FI 103 A1 RE1 - This version was developed between the end of 1944 and the beginning of 1945 to be launched on Holland. The radius of action had been brought to 300 km with the addition of a larger petrol tank at the expense of the explosive charge which had been reduced.

- FI 103 D-1 - Intesa to use chemical weapons, but was not made.

- RE Reichenberg I and II - seater without engine, was towed like a glider.

- Reichenberg RE III - A two-seater with Pulsejet, scheduled for training.

- Reichenberg RE IV - seater with Pulsejet. This was the version that was to become operational. It will be built in more than 175 pieces which, however, will never be put into service.

Towards the end of the conflict were built a number of V1 equipped with a cockpit, modified to allow control by the pilots of volunteers, known as Reichenberg. None of these was used in combat missions. Such airplanes maintained the general characteristics of the bomb from which were derived but unlike the V-1, the take-off did not occur through the launch pad but using the mother aircraft, with release in flight. After an initial phase of development and flight test, he manifested a problem that the technical department could not explain: several test pilots called to test in flight characteristics of the aircraft were killed because they were not able to accomplish the maneuver landing. To try to resolve the anomaly was contacted Hanna Reitsch, who started a series of test flights in order to find the cause. The Reitsch carried out a series of high-altitude simulated landings, repeating suggested for landing using the airspace to have time to recall the aircraft, discovering that the Fi 103R had a very high stall speed and that the above pilots , who had no high-speed flight experience, faced this phase with too low a speed. His recommendation was therefore to maintain a speed of much higher landing maneuver then introduced in the formation of Leonidas Squadron, volunteers pilots destined for 5.Staffel of Kampfgeschwader 200, also known as Leonidas Squadron. Mission planning, then never put into practice, included the use of the Arado Ar 234 jet bomber or as aircraft towing, connected to Reichenberg with a rope, or a mistel-reversed configuration with the aircraft resting on its back. In this configuration, a hydraulic control device operated by the rider had the task of raising the Fi 103R of about eight meters from his home, which is necessary to prevent damage to the upper part of the plane when it was turned on its mother pulsogetto Argus as 014 and to ensure an airflow free from turbulence caused by jet engines Ar 234. a less ambitious project concerned an adaptation to the ventral fuel tank to match the fighters Messerschmitt Me 262. in this case the motor as 014 , internal systems and the head were removed leaving only the wings and the cell now only contained a large tank. A small cylindrical module, similar in shape to a dart finless, was placed on top of the vertical stabilizer at the rear part of the tank and served as a center of balance of gravity and the point of attachment for a variety of equipment. They were provided to connect the two aircraft a rigid tow bar and, at the front end, a pivot pitch. The use of this unusual configuration provided for the adoption of a cart with wheels, connected below to V1-tank to facilitate take-off and peeling off once in flight. Upon exhaustion of the fuel, it was separated from the tow bar through a series of explosive bolts. In 1944 it was conducted a series of tests in flight, however, experiencing a serious problem of the tank structure which tended to "porpoising", instability that is transferred also to the hunting, making the pairing too unreliable to be used. It was also attempted a similar combination with the Arado Ar 234 but up again in the same drawback development was abandoned even in this case. On some of these V1-tank was pioneered the adoption of a showy fixed undercarriage fairing but, in addition to being useless, it helped to increase the aerodynamic drag as well as worsen the overall stability of the whole. One of the original design option Fi 103 reached the operational use. Since 1944, due to the progressive loss of the launch sites in French territory and the general reduction of the area under German control, soon the V1 lost its ability to achieve its targets in England. Although it was developed the dell'aviolancio possibility, he is planned a development able to increase the range of the bomb, identified as F1. It intervened on the weapon tank capacity is larger, with a corresponding reduction of the head mass. Moreover, it was replaced the front of the fuselage, which in V-1 was metallic, with a nose cone in wood, solution that offered a significant weight saving. With these changes the V1 could reach London and the nearby urban centers from locations in the Netherlands. Was given the highest priority to build a number of F1 sufficient to ensure a large bombing campaign to coincide at the beginning of the Ardennes Offensive, but several factors (the bombing of factories producing missiles, the scarcity of available steel, network failure for their rail transport, chaotic tactical situation that Germany was facing at the time of the conflict, etc.) delayed delivery of this V-1 making himself available only between February and March 1945. Before the campaign attack based on the V-1 was finally ended in late March, were several hundred F1 who reached Britain launched by the Dutch sites. An example is the Imperial War Museum in London. Also in London for another copy it is located at the Science Museum. In Paris, however, it can be admired at the Musée de l'Armée. The V-1 was also copied by others, for example by the US Navy who intended to make a bombing system against Japanese coast, the Willys-Overland JB-2 / KGW / KUW / LTV-A-1 / LTV-N-2 Loon, which was developed from July 1944, when the wreckage of a V1 were brought to the USA. The new bomb it took many months to be considered reliable, but the USAAF put into practice a radio guidance system with a 'beacon' radar to help locate the missile and final radio command to the dive; it was estimated that this could improve the precision, and at 160 km effects were obtained 400 m, at least an order of magnitude greater. Also launches were made from a B-17 and were placed orders for 75,000 missiles, but the invasion of Japan there was. The 'Thunderbug', so named dall'USAAF, was completed in 1,391 copies. In December 1944 they failed launches 8 out of ten; but in June they went well 128 of 164, while it was estimated to produce between 1,000 and 5,000 per month. This was not a result of induced weapon 'bankruptcy' as painting the Allied propaganda. The US Navy instead wanted to launch them from the escort carrier, but later experienced the two submarines, contributing to the development of the Regulus missile. The characteristics of the Loon were: weight 2,270 kg, 907 kg of warhead, pulsogetto from 360 kgs, speed of 685 km / h.

Technical features

Dimensions and weights

- Weight: 2,150 kg
- Length: 8,32 meters
- Height: 1.42 meters

performance

- Vectors: Heinkel He 111
- Range: 250 km
- Tangent: 2,750 meters (theoretical)
- Maximum speed: 640 km / h
- Engine: a pulsogetto Argus As 014
- Head: 830 kg
- Blast: amatol-39 or Danarit
- Fuel: 80 octane petrol
- Cost: $ 500

Fieseler Fi 103R

The Fieseler Fi 103R, initially known as Reichenberg, was an average military wing single-seater aircraft defined as piloted flying bomb, German company Fieseler GmbH in the forties. It was a pilot version of Wunderwaffe V-1. Developed as supplied to the voluntary special ward of the Luftwaffe 5.Staffel of Kampfgeschwader 200, also known as Leonidas Squadron, he was part of a kamikaze mission program planned in the last phase of World War II but never entered the operational phase. Towards the end of World War II the adverse war situation to Nazi Germany grew more and more worrying and it became necessary by military authorities to urge the arms industry to find a solution to reverse the tide. In this context it was also evaluated the possibility of setting up special units composed of volunteer pilots able to make its own contribution in suicide operational missions. To do this, on direct suggestion of Adolf Hitler, it was created a new squadron framed within the kampfgeschwader 200, the 5.Staffel better known as Leonidas Squadron, where riders were required to sign a document that stated: *"With this voluntarily ask to be enrolled in the suicide group as part of a glider-piloting a human bomb. I fully understand that the operational use in this capacity will result in my death."*

As equipment were initially considered for both the Messerschmitt Me 328 that the Fieseler Fi 103 (better known as suitably modified V-1 flying bomb), but after a comparative evaluation is preferred to the first paired with a 900 kg bomb. However, the conversion proved difficult to the point that Heinrich Himmler thought it was more appropriate to cancel the project. Hitler, however, convinced of the department, to relaunch the activities contacted Otto Skorzeny, thanks to the experience gained in the studies regarding the possibility of using manned torpedoes against Allied naval units. They were begun feasibility studies on the V-1 which was given the code name "Projekt Reichenberg" (from Reichenberg, the capital of the historical region Czechoslovak Sudetenland, now known as Liberec). The development of the "Reichenberg-Geräte" (Reichenberg equipment), as it was called the Fi 103R, concerned a series of changes to the V1, the most striking of which was the adoption of a cockpit closed by a removable windshield, solution which it was preferred to give anyway an opportunity of salvation to the pilot involved in the mission of attack. In the summer of 1944, the Deutsche Forschungsanstalt für Segelflug (DFS), the research institute for gliding based in Ainring, took on the task of developing the pilot version of the V1 putting into place in only a few days a specimen to be allocated to the tests and to install a production line at Dannenberg. The V1 was transformed in Reichenberg by inserting into the cell a small cabin in the position immediately in front of the air intake of pulsogetto, where the V-1 standards were inserted compressed air tanks. The cockpit was basic, with a minimum of flight instrumentation and a bucket seat made of plywood, closed by a sunroof, made in a single piece, which incorporated a front armored panel and a side opening to allow access to the pilot. The two compressed air tanks were replaced by a single one, mounted in the back, going to occupy the space that normally housed in the V1 on autopilot. The wings were modified by incorporating metal edges can cut the cables of barrage balloons. The proposal was that the aircraft was being transported by an airplane mother, a Heinkel He 111 bomber, capable of locks on one or two under the wings and dropping them into the vicinity of the target. The pilot would take him on the objective, dropping the little roof before reaching it and parachute jumping. However, the proximity of the engine air intake compromised the ease of operation to the point that the calculation of the percentage of survival of the pilots appeared around 1%. Pilot training began on conventional gliders, to give them the ability to handle the airship during gliding, then continuing on special gliders, modified by one sail from reduced wingspan and be able to perform maneuvers beaten reaching 300 km / h.

A specimen of Selbstopfer, a Fieseler Fi 103.

The third phase involved the R-II education, two-seat variant of Reichenberg. Advanced training was carried out on the RI and R-II and although the landing maneuver on proved difficult ventral shoe, the models were to have a good flight behavior for which he suggested that the Leonidas Squadron, volunteers drivers for the Leonidas Squadron, they could soon be able to carry out operational missions. Albert Speer, in a dispatch sent to Hitler July 28, 1944, suggested not to waste of resources and targets men on French soil and that they would be more effective against Soviet territory in electric power plants. For what can be considered the first real flight to wait until September 1944, when a Reichenberg was disconnected from a He 111 in the sky above Larz. The flight, however, proved to be a failure because the aircraft crashed after the pilot had lost control due to the accidental actuation of the fairing separation device. Auks the second flight, carried out the following day, ended with an accident. The incidents followed one another, a problem which the technical department could not explain: several test pilots called to test in flight characteristics of the aircraft were killed because they were unable to make a landing maneuver. To try to resolve the anomaly were contacted Heinz Kensche and Hanna Reitsch who started a series of test flights in order to find the cause. Both were stars of any accidents from which still came out unscathed. On November 5, 1944 during the second flight of the R-III test, a wing broke away due to vibration however Kensche managed to operate the safety parachute albeit with some difficulty due to the small size of the passenger. The Reitsch carried out a series of high-altitude simulated landings, repeating suggested for landing using the airspace to have time to recall the aircraft, discovering that the Fi 103R had a very high stall speed and that the above pilots , who had no high-speed flight experience, faced this phase with too low a speed. His recommendation was therefore to maintain a landing speed much higher, maneuver then introduced into the Leonidas Squadron formation. After Werner Baumbach took command of the KG 200, in October 1944, he took the decision to shelve the development of Reichenberg in favor of the Mistel project. Baumbach and Speer finally managed to have a meeting with Hitler March 15, 1945 where he argued that the suicide missions were not part of the German military traditions, convincing him to approve their suspension. Later that same day, Baumbach ordered the dissolution unit Reichenberg.

Bachem Ba 349

The Bachem Ba 349 Natter (in German "Viper") was an experimental interceptor equipped with rocket propulsion made by the German company Bachem-Werke GmbH in the forties and used operationally, in a very similar way to air missiles, in the final stages of World war II. Most of the flight until the bombers was guided by radio control from the ground and the pilot was then landing with a parachute. Made with a limited use of strategic materials, the aircraft was one of Wunderwaffe developed to try to subvert the German decline in the evolution of the conflict. With air superiority of the Luftwaffe made serious test by the Allies over the skies of the Reich in 1943, to prevent the crisis were demands of radical innovations. The air missiles appeared to be a very promising approach to counter the offensive of the Allied bombers and was kicked off on several projects, but various problems with the guidance system prevented a large-scale use of the latter. Equip the missile of a pilot who would have been able to control the weapon during the critical final phase of the flight it seemed to be the best solution, and this specification was required by the Luftwaffe at the beginning of 1944.

A large number of simple designs were proposed, most of which provided for the rider in a prone position to reduce the front section. The main candidate to specific was initially the Heinkel P.1077 taking off from a launch pad and landed on a slide just as the Messerschmitt Me 163 Komet. The BP20 Erich Bachem was a development from a project on which he was working at Fieseler, but considerably more radical of the other proposals. It was constructed using pieces of wood glued and screwed on an armored passenger compartment, driven by a rocket Walter HWK 109-509A-2 liquid propellant, similar to the ME 163. Four rockets releasable Schmidding were employed for take-off, for a boost total of 4,800 kgf (47 kN) for 10 seconds after being launched. The plane interupted by a ramp of about 25 meters, necessary for achieving a sufficient speed to operate the aerodynamic controls to be able to control it. The plane took off and was driven from the ground up to the altitude of the Allied bombers by radio control, with the driver who took control only for the time necessary to point the muzzle in the right direction, loosen the plastic hull and pull the trigger. The latter fired a salvo of rockets (33 R4M or 24 Hs 217), after which the plane was flying over the bombers. After exhausting the propellant, the aircraft had to be used to hit the tail of a bomber, with the pilot parachuted to the ground just before impact. Despite its apparent complexity, the project had a decisive advantage over rivals: eliminated the need to land a rocket-fast plane at an airbase that, as demonstrated by the history of ME 163, was extremely vulnerable to raids of Allied planes . After the draft Bachem had attracted the attention of Heinrich Himmler to the SS command, he became the official winner of the specification. The Luftwaffe, however, planned to include some minor renovations to try to save the plane can, for example, eliminating the final attack to impact. The resulting small air would have to be fired from a wooden ramp of 15 meters with the help of four rockets solid propulsion, at the end of which he reached the speed required to operate its control surfaces. The rockets would be turned off after 12 seconds, after which the main engine would be brought to the maximum thrust. At this point the mission was supposed to bring the aircraft to a position in front and over the enemy bombers, where the pilot would have switched off the autopilot, and it would come down to an attack on plane. After firing its armament of rockets he would continue to high-speed glide up to an altitude of 3,000 meters, after which the aircraft would be "broken" due to the opening of a large parachute on the back of the aircraft, separating it from the front with the pilot. Both sides would be landed with their different parachutes, and the fuselage with wooden wings would have been lost. The models for wind tunnel that had been built at the beginning of the program were sent elsewhere for testing and the results returned to the designers of Bachem indicated that it would be "satisfactory" for speeds of less than 1,100 km/h.

A Bachem Ba349, with open cockpit and the bow rockets on display.

life-sized models were then completed and began test flights in November 1944. Early versions did not include any engine, and then pulled into the air by a bomber Heinkel He 111 for testing soaring. Additional test launch and autopilot were made with solid propulsion engines. All had a positive outcome, but it became apparent that it would not be possible to reuse the engine; the landing speed was simply too high. The construction of models of production Ba 349A had already begun in October, and fifteen of them were launched in the next few months. Each launch involved a slight modification of the design, and eventually these were collected in the final version of production, Ba 349B which began testing in January. US forces seized the factory Waldsee in April, but some of the staff of Bachem managed to escape taking with him the ten Series B remaining aircraft Soon, however, the Americans were able to catch them, and six of the ten aircraft were given to flames. In February 1945, the SS established that the program was not progressing fast enough, and ordered an operational launch by the end of the month. The first and only time that the plane was tested in this way was on February 28, when Lothar Sieber flew on a Ba 349A, which was launched from the area of military training near Stetten am kalten Markt. At first, everything seemed to go as planned, but at 500 meters above sea level the hood pulled away. The aircraft, having turned on its back, first climbed to 1,500 meters, and then fell to the ground. Sieber died in the accident, and was never identified the cause. He was suspected that the hood had not been properly fixed before launch. Some sources claim that an operating unit of Natter was prepared by volunteers in Kirchheim unter Teck, but were unable to complete any transaction. However there is no evidence for this version, which seems somewhat risky. In the Hasenholz forest near Kirchheim unter Teck we had three launching pads for the Bachem Ba 349 and are all that remains from an active launch site was built in 1945. The three launch pads are arranged in the shape of an equilateral triangle, the sides of which point towards the east and south. The distance between the ramps is approximately 50 meters. The circular platforms on which once stood the Bachem Ba 349 and their launch towers still exist today. In the center of each of them there is a deep square hole about 50 centimeters, which served as the foundation for the launch pad. Next to each hole there is a ramp, cut to the ground level, which probably once served as the connecting hole. The launching sites of Natter in Kirchheim (Teck) may be the only remaining of areas still accessible to the public. The first test site for Natter in Baden-Württemberg near Stetten am kalten Markt is still a military area in use, and therefore is not accessible to tourists.

Technical features

- Length: 6,02 meters
- Wingspan: 3.60 meters
- Height: 2.25 meters
- Wing area: 2,75 m²
- Empty weight: 880 kg
- Maximum takeoff weight: 2,232 kg
- Engine: Engine Walter HWK 109-509A-2 with

Four solid rocket boosters
- Thrust 16.7 kN (1,700 kg)
- Top speed: 800 km / h at sea level - 1000 km / h at high altitude
- Service Ceiling: 14,000 meters
- Missiles: 24 Hs 217 Föhn rockets from 73 mm or 33 rockets R4M 55 mm weighing 3.5 kg each and a maximum speed of 525 meters per second.

Mistel Project

The designated Mistel composite aircraft were conceived in Nazi Germany and used by the Special kampfgeschwader 200 to bomb specific targets, thanks to the unusual combination of two planes together.

The idea involved the joint launch of the two components, then headed toward the goal by the element upper unit, with the pilot above the lens, he would release the lower plane, while continuing to drive it via a remote link up to crash it into the lens. The combination most used foresaw a fighter plane as a vector to which it was attached, through a system of cables and specially designed connections, a Junkers Ju 88 bomber like the bottom, with a head full of explosives in place of the passenger compartment. The Mistel 1 had, for the accuracy, as a specimen of the Bf 109 F-4 version, and as the Ju 88 night fighters version well with 8,377 pounds of explosive, capable of drilling well 8 meters of steel and / or 20 meters reinforced concrete. As the upper part, following the Mistel series he was chosen the Focke-Wulf Fw 190. He brought out the form 2. At one point it was decided to resort to heavy bombers Heinkel He 177 as a lower element, given the uselessness of these aircraft for the Reich. The hunt brought in an accentuated beat the bomber and unhooked from it by detonating explosives placed electrically spherical joints on the main side members. The fighters were removed the machine guns mounted on the wings but were still left mounted machine guns / cannons fuselage. Quill shock had settled into a long trunk, so do gradually explode the nose cone shaped charge before the bomber was going to crash completely against the target.

The Mistel could touch 380 km / h. The unit authorized to use the Mistel was kampfgeschwader 200, KG 200-200° flock bombers, who employed him for the first time against the Allied troops during the Battle of Normandy, June 24, 1944. The attack, carried out at damage of boats anchored between Cherbourg and Le Havre, was successful and some ships were sunk. By early 1945 it was planned a mass of Mistel attack against electric nearby stations in Moscow that was estimated by the Germans, distributed energy to about 80% of Soviet war, but a daytime raid destroyed USAAF many Mistel ground before they could take off and consequently the mission was canceled. Success was instead the attack of March 6, 1945 where the KG 200 used the Mistel to destroy two bridges over the Oder River in Göritz, to slow the Red Army march to Berlin. The first raid took place on the day of the Mistel March 8, 1945 against the Goritz bridge over the Oder destroying the bridge (two aircraft), one destroyed the flak, one did not work. The second raid took place March 31, 1945, where it was destroyed the railway bridge of Steinau, The raid forced the Red Army to slow the onslaught in Berlin a few days.

Versions

- Mistel Prototyp: prototype consists of a Ju 88 A-4 and a Bf 109 F-4 fighter.
- Mistel 1: standard version consists of a Ju 88 A-4 and a Bf 109 F-4, one of the two actually used in operational missions.
- Mistel S1: trainer version of the Mistel 1.
- Mistel 2: composition of a Ju 88 G-l and a fighter Fw 190 A-8 or F-8.
- Mistel S2: trainer version of the Mistel 2.
- Mistel 3rd: composition between a Ju 88 A-4 and a fighter Fw 190 A-8, one of the two actually used in operational missions.
- Mistel S3A: from the Mistel 3A trainer version.

- Mistel 3B: composition between a Ju 88 H-4 and a fighter Fw 190 A-8.
- Mistel 3C: composition between a Ju 88 G-10 and a fighter Fw 190 F-8.
- Mistel 3rd: composition between a Ju 88 A-4 and a fighter Fw 190 A-8.
- Mistel Führungsmaschine: composition between a Ju 88 A-4 / H-4 and a fighter Fw 190 A-8.
- Mistel 4: composition of a Junkers Ju 287 and a Messerschmitt Me 262.
- Mistel 5: also known by the designation RLM Junkers Ju 268, composition between a Arado E 377 A and an interceptor fighter Heinkel He 162 remained at the planning stage.

The V2

The V2 rocket was the forerunner of ballistic missiles and was widely used by Germany during the latter stages of World War II, particularly against Great Britain and Belgium. V2 is the acronym for Vergeltungswaffe 2 (retaliatory weapon 2 in German, an idea of Joseph Goebbels for propaganda purposes).
The missile was designated by its designers as A4 (Aggregat 4). Already since 1927, members of the German Society began the first tests on liquid-fueled rockets. In 1932, the Reichswehr (the German National Defense) was interested in the developments of these tests especially for the military, and a team led by General Walter Dornberger was greatly impressed by a carrier test designed and built by Wernher von Braun. Despite the characteristics of this first rocket were very limited, Dornberger was able to guess the genius of von Braun and then urged him to join the army in order to continue the development of its research. Von Braun accepted, as did many other members of society. The A-4 / V-2 was inintercettabile. A weapon against which there was no defense. To date, only a deployment of Patriot or SA-10 could pararne the attack, and at enormous cost, against this it was an ancestor of the current Scud, similar in performance and tested but more precise and weighing half. On 6 September 1944, when the V-1 missiles were already beginning to wane, the V-2 launches began against Paris, m without success; 8 instead began to hit London. Their arrival had no warning signs, no alarms and whistles. The government did believe that it was a gas leak, but soon had to admit the threat. People are not bad taken, because it was more fatalistic view explode from time to time a palace than suffer the terror of sirens and antiaircraft, and clusters of bombs falling from the

sky. Londoners continued to hope for the victory and resisted, even though they had thousands of victims.

The only sighted weapon in the air by a Spitfire, which veered and he went on the attack, in less than no time had disappeared in the clouds. However, launch the V2 was not easy; there were over 100 tonnes to carry around to launch such weapons; They were to erect after having mounted the cylinder head, which contained Amatol, little powerful explosive but stable seen that the re-entry into the most powerful explosives would explode, as often happened, despite the thick fiber glass structure used for insulation. The next step was to build the weapon with the head of a reusable metal platform (up to a dozen times), and then supplying the bomb with 4,173 kg of ethyl alcohol and 5.533 kg of oxygen. It was hard, almost as if it were an experimental program rather than an operational weapon, and it was dangerous if there were problems, for example if it drew a strong side wind. The preparation for the launch of the V-2 was difficult, and required 28-30 support vehicles. A whole other world than the single truck high mobility of the descendants evolved 'Scud'.

The missile was ready after work hours and you had to be careful with the air strikes, with Typhoon always around at low altitude, as the radius of the V-2 was limited and could not be increased a lot. The weapon was not very precise, about 4 km from the center of the target, but it was a bit 'better, however, the V-1. The latter was trappable, but after all carried roughly the same charge on the same distances, but with a weight and a much lower cost, as well as with a system easier to produce and use. Later they came even think of V-2 launchable from special containers towed by submarines, and even V-2 with wings, ingenious system but difficult to implement to better exploit the energy weapon. To the point, the dell'endoreattore potential, operated with 730 hp turbo pump from that mixed in the combustion chamber components, while the jet was diverted with graphite panels according to the internal stabilized platform which was the guidance system, was exploited for a long time; even the colossal rockets of the type R-7 Semyorka Soviets were still based on that type of endoreattore, with 20 engines mounted in parallel to form a more powerful; and despite the complication, the complex used by the Soviets has proven to work with remarkable reliability. Connected to the V-2 Rocket was the U-boat, a secret German military project to create the first ballistic missile submarine capable of launching SLBMs (English acronym that means Submarine-launched ballistic missile that is "ballistic missile from submarine") . The idea, later abandoned, was conceived by the Nazi Third Reich during World War II. The original plan called for the use of German U-boats to attack the city of New York through the use of new missiles V2. In 1941 he was decided to adapt the unit U-511 of the class U-Boot Type IX-C, which already from the first experiments had confirmed the validity of the idea, being able to escape the missiles from its upper part, both in emergence, both in immersion up to an altitude of 12 meters; However, at that time Germany was more concentrated on the development of the V1, and so this project was put aside. In 1943 the project was revived after the V1 had reached the operational stage; Once again, however, the project to use the V1 on a U-boat was shelved. He went back to talk about this project in 1943-44 in most advanced form, planning the attack in New York: name Prüfstand code XII; for this mission you wanted to use the V2 missiles, submarines but were not able to accommodate them, and then it was decided to switch to another solution, namely, mount the V-2 within a large watertight cylindrical container it would be towed across the Atlantic. After reaching its launch position, the V-2 was launched on New York. To this end it was thought to use the Type XXI submarine, which would have drawn three containers across the Atlantic, containers which in addition to the V-2 would have contained also the reserve of fuel (diesel fuel), intended to supply the submarine during the his journey. To launch the missile, the ballast tanks in the container would be flooded, bringing it in a vertical position to be launched towards his goal.

U-Boot type XXI at anchor as a museum ship.

However, the allies were aware of Germany's missile program and had drawn up a contingency plan, codenamed Operation Teardrop, which was to use four groups of aircraft carriers to prevent the penetration of U-Boot on American shores; and, in fact, in March 1945, a group of six U-Boot Type IX-C was intercepted along the American and four submarines coasts were sunk, even if it was established that it was not a missile attack with V-2.

Technology

The rocket A1 was the first of Aggregat series. It was designed in 1933 by Wernher von Braun as part of a research program of the Wehrmacht at Kummersdorf, under the guidance of Walter Dornberger.

From a technical standpoint, this rocket was 1.4 meters long, with a diameter of 0.3. The launch weight was 150 kg, of which 40 constituted by the fuel, a mixture of liquid oxygen and alcohol (75%). The engine would have to ensure a 16-second operation. The pressure engine designed by Rudolph had to provide 300 kg of thrust for 16 seconds: the prototype exploded on the launching pad, and the project was abandoned because it was considered unstable. Consequently, the project came to nothing, but formed the basis of the more perfected A2.

In December of 1934 was another successful missile A-2, a small rocket engine with ethanol and liquid oxygen. The rocket A2 was the first flying test of the program that would later become the V2.

Altogether, there were launched two, both in 1934, 19 and 20 December, which were called, respectively, with the names in the code of Max and Moritz, who reached respectively 2.2 km and 3.5 km high.

This was a rather small system, little longer A1, 1,61 meters long and 0.31 in diameter. The launch weight was 107 kg, of which 35 of propellant (the same mixture of A1

LOX-alcohol). Since 1936, the group led by von Braun concentrated on the construction of the rocket successors A-2, A-3 and A-4.

The A3 formed the first large rocket designed by von Braun and his team.

From a technical standpoint, it was a long 6.74 meter system, with a diameter of 0.67 and a width of 0.93. The launch weight was 740 kg and the engine was fueled by the usual mixture LOX-alcohol, with an operating time of 45 seconds and a pressure of 1,500 kg.

Furthermore, within the liquid oxygen tanks, it had been mounted one containing liquid nitrogen: this was electrically heated, thereby producing nitrogen in the gaseous state to the pressurization of the propellant.

This rocket, also, was equipped with a guidance system consists of three gyroscopes and two accelerometers. He completed equipping a small camera placed on the nose of the missile. The A3, however, constituted a complete failure, since he could not even one of the four test launches were performed between 4 and 11 December 1937. As a result, what should have been a small-scale model of the final and more powerful A4, the future V2, had to be completely redesigned. The A4 was the first rocket propellant liquid to enter into operational service. Better known by the name of propaganda V2 (Vergeltungswaffe 2 or retaliatory weapon 2), it was built in about 6,000 copies, and was the basis for the US missile programs, French and Soviet. The development, in practice, was launched by von Braun in the early thirties, and were made a large number of flying testbeds and demonstrators technologies (A1, A2, A3 and A5).

The first launch was carried out March 23, 1942 at the Peenemunde site, with the entrance in regular service since 1944.

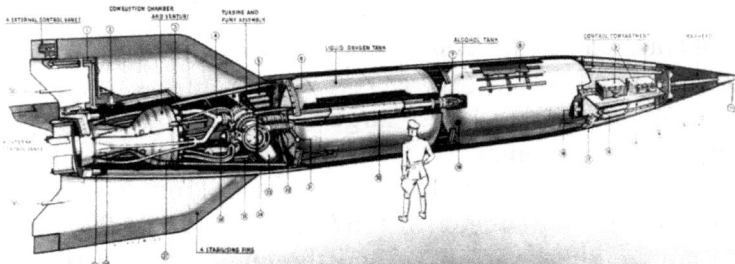

From a technical standpoint, it was a heavy liquid rocket to the launch of 12,805 kg, with:

- Length: 14 meters.
- Diameter: 1.65 meters.
- Motor: from 730 hp power, 26,000 kgs of thrust at sea level.
- explosive load: about 1 ton of Amatol or Nippolit.
- Range: between 320 and 360 kilometers.
- Approximate speed, five thousand kilometers per hour.
- Ballast: 4 tons.
- take off weight: 12 tonnes.
- Fuel Weight:
  - Liquid oxygen: 4.7 tons
  - Alcohol: 2.7 tons.
- Liquid Weight of the turbopump:
  - 0.0076 tons of potassium permanganate.
  - 0,175 tons of hydrogen peroxide.
  - The mixture of these two liquids produced a vapor that is mixed in the combustion chamber by liquid oxygen and alcohol sent under pressure.

Besides the "classic" version, can be executed from the ground, they were proposed for use by a submarine (abandoned due to technical problems in 1944), an anti-aircraft (Wasserfall, actually launched) and provided with wings with increased output and possibility of human pilot (A4b, launched in duplicate, unmanned).

Engine of V2.

The A5 constituted a test on a small scale of what would become the final V2. Made in place of bankruptcy A3, it presented several differences compared to this, including the aerodynamic forms and the control system. The propulsion plant, however, was the same. In general, it was a system along 5.82 meters, with a diameter of 0.78 and a launch weight of 900 kg. However, they were carried out different variations in experiments, which could be launched by parachute, or used a monopropellant propulsion of the type system. 70 were produced, of which 25 without motor or monopropellant rocket to test the aerodynamics launched from airplanes, all parachute to soften the landing: floated up to two hours to allow recovery at sea. The launches were carried out between 1938 and 1942. With the need to test the A-3 and then subsequently the A-4, it was clear that von Braun projects were becoming reality, so the General Dornberger, on the advice of the mother of von Braun, moved the team from Kummersdorf (near Berlin) to a small town, Peenemünde, on the island of Usedom, Baltic coast of Germany, to provide better technical infrastructure / logistics for tests and also get greater privacy. The rocket A-3 proved unreliable when practical, so it was decided to completely overhaul the development of this model under the name of a new project called A-5. This new version was much more reliable, and in 1941 about 70 rockets had been tested A-5. The first operational missile A-4 flew in March 1942 and covered only a path of 1.5 km, then crashing into the sea. The second launch had more luck, reached an altitude of about 11 km before exploding. The third launch, on 3 October 1942 it was instead crowned with complete success: the missile A-4 followed almost a perfect trajectory and crashed 193 km away from the launch pad exceeding 80 km altitude. The production of A-4 started in 1943, however its use in war was not entirely a surprise for the allies, as these were already in German weapon knowledge. In fact, later in one of the many A-4 test, in Poland, a missile had been recovered from militants of the Polish resistance and the technical details were then transmitted to the British secret service.

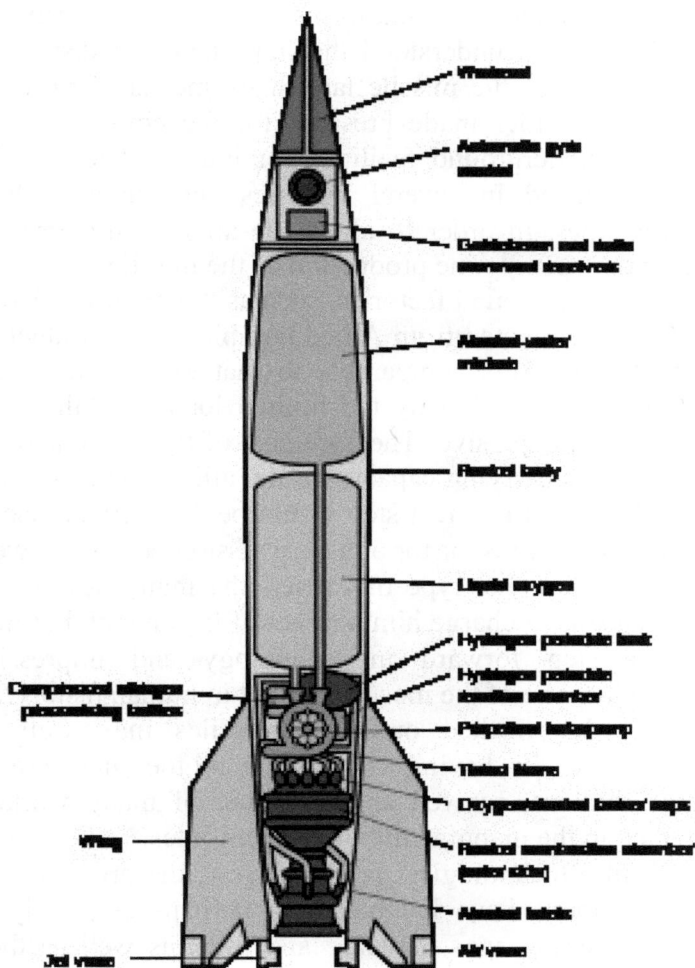

At this point, for the British, it was clear that the new threat was looming on the horizon and then launched a major offensive against the construction of the complex A-4. In particular, the base of Peenemünde was heavily bombed in July 1943, causing delays in the production of missiles and the death of many technicians and workers, among which there were also some inmates of a concentration camp near. Meanwhile, also in 1943, the V2 were adoperate as platforms for remote sensing. Dornberger had understood the importance of dispersing the complex of the missile launch by means of movable ramps, but Hitler made pressure for the construction of immense underground facilities for launch. The missiles were produced in several factories and shipped along railway lines, in order to allow the almost uninterrupted hurl at the enemy. The production of the missile took place in large underground factories, such as the notorious Dora-Mittelbau, protected from Allied bombing. The production cost of a V2 was comparable to that of a bomber and certainly not justified by the limited load (less than one ton) of high explosive. The high cost of the bomb and the Joint limited carrying capacity of the allied secret services did believe that the next step would be the German use of the missile as a vector for a nuclear fission bomb. V2 were not simply another type of carrier, the many devised, to launch a war to charge him a target of the enemy, but they were a step forward in technology and impressive knowledge, one of the most important in human history.

People who worked on these missiles may well be remembered for having contributed to the massacre of many civilians, as well as the killing of many workers detained in the manufacture of these missiles.

But from a technological point of view, the progress that these weapons have led both and perhaps especially in scientific terms, was immense and they, as well as their technicians who have continued to work in the most important countries, have formed the backbone era missile, a key part of our present civilization. The Aggregat used a mixture of ethanol (75%) and water (25%) said B-Stoff or Hydrazine as fuel and liquid oxygen (A-Stoff) as combustion, about 1,200 pumped through small holes into the combustion chamber (or furnace) for optimize the mix, respectively 74% and 26%. Hydrazine passed around before the furnace to cool (and warm the hydrazine), a regenerative cooling theorized by Tsiolkovsky and Goddard and designed by Eugene Sanger for Silbervogel: the process limited the furnace temperature to 2500-2700 degrees combustion . The injection into the furnace was via a turbo pump powered by steam produced from a 66% solution of sodium permanganate and hydrogen peroxide (80%), similar to the Walther Kriegsmarine engines. The Hydrazine was made to run down the furnace to reduce the temperature at the exit, and its combustion caused the long white feather of typical fumes of the first V-2. The turbopump reduced the pressure required for the tanks of A-and B-Stoff Stoff, which gave 65 seconds of maximum autonomy, allowing the A-4 to reach in average of 80 km or even more to inertia. The launch positions were studied to know the distance and the azimuth of the target: the fin 1 was aligned with the azimuth, and the LEV-3 guidance system (the most used) was adjusted with distance. The LEV-3 was an inertial system with a horizontal and a vertical gyro to stabilize the missile and a PIGA (Integrating pendulous gyroscopic Accelerometer) to stop the engine at the desired distance. In 20% of the V-2 were used as the radio controls Leitstrahl that by bunkers along the way received pulses to adjust the route of the missiles. The PIGA was invented by Fritz Mueller specifically for the V-2; It was substantially axial to a gyroscope rocket, with a tilting electric contact. By turning on the axis opened a contact and started a twisting motor that controlled the fins counter the rotation. The rotation of the base was used to calculate the speed, and then the time to turn off the engine and start the fall.

The A6 was the designation which gave the men of von Braun to the project of a missile driven by photographic reconnaissance which was, for its characteristics in terms of performance, practically invulnerable. From a technical standpoint, the study, carried out in 1943, was based on a test bench A5 version with the propulsion system consists of a ramjet. In detail, the project provided a rocket with human pilot 15.75 meters long, with a diameter of 6.33, which was to be launched vertically. After the launch, it was expected to reach a maximum altitude of 95 km, with the return in the atmosphere with a planing speed supersonic. Subsequently, it would take place the ignition of the engine, the said ramjet, which would have to maintain a speed of 2,900 km / h for 15-20 minutes. For landing, it was foreseen the use of a parachute or a normal airport. In Germany, this project was presented to the German Air Ministry, however, not having the need for an aircraft like that, she turned it down. After the war, however, both the United States and the Soviet Union used a similar configuration, but not driven, for the construction of cruise missiles with ramjet SM-64 Navaho and Burya. The A7 was supposed to be a demonstrator scaled-tech rocket A9. However, it was never built, and the work was interrupted in 1940. However, it would have dealt a rocket 5,91 meters long, with a diameter of 0.38 and a weight of 1,000 kg. The A8 was the project on a stretched version of the V2, which should have used storable propellants. This system was developed in 1941, but was never initiated the construction of a prototype or a demonstrator. However, after the war, continued his studies at the hands of the French, in relation to the so-called Super V-2: it was an IRBM, then canceled because too ambitious, but which formed the basis for the missiles Veronique, Diamant and, distantly, to the Ariane launch vehicle. The A9 was the project for a rocket plane that was carried out in 1944. It was, in effect, a version with a human pilot and fitted with the V2 wings, the development of which, however, was banned by the high command. Despite this, however, von Braun continued to work on this project, which received the internal code name of A4b. This aircraft flew two copies. According to the designers' intentions, this system would have had a launch weight of 16,259 kg, of which 1,000 of payload, with a length of 14.18 meters and a diameter of 3.2, and would be able to carry his load at 600 km of distance 17 minutes after launch.

Another variant of the A9, unmanned, was developed to be used as a second stage on ballistic missile A9 / A10.

The A9 / A10 was the project for a two-stage intercontinental ballistic missile with an estimated range of around 5,000 kilometers. The development of this weapon system was started in 1940, with the provision of a first flight in 1946. The project, however, was blocked for orders over in 1943, when it was decided to concentrate all efforts on the V2. Von Braun, however, continued to work to the missile, in particular to the second stage (A9), which was tested with the denomination of A4b. Only at the end of 1944, Von Braun and his team were officially allowed to resume research on this strategic weapon system, which received encoding Projekt Amerika (America Project). However, this weapon at long range and had absolutely no practical development: the only real evidence riguardarono dell'A4b two flights, the last of which in January 1945.

The A9 / A10 should have been a two-stage missile with liquid propellant (LOX and alcohol), with a launch weight greater than 85 tons and can carry a 1,000 kg warhead to 5,000 km. The name of the missile was due, essentially, to that of the two stages, which were called, precisely, A9 and A10. Of these two stages, during the development phase, it was hypothesized various configurations.

- A10: it was the first stage of the missile. In its original version, he should have had an engine consists of a cluster of six combustion chambers of A4, liquid propellant (LOX / alcohol), with a single exhaust nozzle. Subsequently, it was decided to use a propeller with a single combustion chamber, larger in size. For the real test of this engine, at the Peenemunde plant were built some test benches. The motor should have a thrust of 200,000 kgf, and a diameter of 4.12 meters.

- A9: it was the second stage of the missile, part of which was also experienced. In its initial configuration, he would have consisted of a normal A4 with two small wings to the side. The experiments were carried sull'A4b, which in practice was a V2 "series" with wings and weight increased. Of this, it was launched two copies, 27 December 1944 and 24 January 1945. The first test failed. Subsequent launches, even though they were expected, were however never carried out because of the disastrous course of the conflict. However, the final configuration of the A9 foresaw a kind of plane rocket with human piloting, characterized by two small lateral wings along the fuselage: this solution, in fact, according to the tests conducted in the wind tunnel, it would have resulted in a whole series of advantages, both during the flight in the supersonic speed, both in terms of assembly with the first stage.

One of the biggest problems that we had to face was that relating to the steering system: the long range, in fact, made of this very imprecise weapon system. For this reason, the designers evaluated the use of the human piloting. According to the planned mission profile, therefore, the A9 would have to be separated from the first stage to an altitude of 390 km and at the speed of 3,400 m / s. Next, it should start a re-entry phase, heading for his goal driven by radio or from submarines in the Atlantic Ocean. The pilot, when you aim the lens, should have blocked the route of the aircraft and eject. The problem was that it was a very risky maneuver: not only, in fact, was potentially deadly, but if successful would have resulted in the safe capture of man to guide the missile. The A9 / A10 / A11 was the project for a three-stage missile, able both to launch a 500 kg artificial satellite in low Earth orbit, it is being used as an intercontinental ballistic missile. Carried out in 1944, it was of the A9 / A10 which should have been added a stadium, the A11, consisting of a cluster of six engines of the A10. As nell'A9 / A10, A9 would have to be provided with wings, so that it can be used in bombing missions or retrieved later. The height of this missile would have to reach the 41.5 meters, with a diameter of 8.1 and a launch weight of 586,000 kg. The estimated apogee was 300 km away. According to the designers, the missile would have to have an overall height of 41 meters, with a diameter of 4.12 and a launch weight of 85,300 kg, of which 1,000 of weapons load. The output, as previously mentioned, would have to reach the 5,000 km away. The A9 / A10 / A11 / A12 was the project for a spacecraft capable of carrying low Earth orbit a payload of 10,000 kg. You would have to have an aircraft in four stages, of which the last three comprise the A9 / A10 / A11 missile, and the first A12. The latter would have to be constituted by a cluster of 50 A10 engines. This project was carried out by von Braun between 1948 and 1952. The reconstructions are purely hypothetical, however, it would have to be a rocket 70 meters high and with a maximum diameter of 11, who weighed 4,100 tons at launch. The benefits provided were a carrying capacity of 10,000 kg to 300 km altitude.

Launch sites

On 18 December 1942, a military deployment plan is processed as a result of Hitler's decision of 22 November that the V2 had to be prepared and launched from fortified installations (bunkers). The first work began in late March 1942 in the following locations:

- Eperlecques - North of France, the department of Pas de Calais.
- Wizernes - North of France, the department of Pas de Calais.
- Sottevast - Northern France, in the Manche department in the Basse-Normandie region.
- Brecourt - the assault on the Brécourt manor was a clash between US paratroopers of the 101st Airborne Division against German troops positioned south of Utah Beach, during the early stages of the Normandy landings, during the second world war.
- Rinxent - North of France, the department of Pas de Calais.
- Caumont - North of France, the department of Calvados, in the Basse-Normandie region.
- Dieppedalle - North of France, the department of Seine-Maritime, in the Haute Normandie region.

Following the numerous operations of bombardment, these sites were subsequently abandoned, despite new construction techniques with a significant increase of their protection, opting for mobile launch sites scattered throughout the region. This new type of launch mode was set in early 1944 as a result of the many air raids. In the northern communities and Pas de Calais they were set up 23 launch sites for V2 in the forests and sometimes in the parks of several castles, far away from prying eyes.

Each launch site was composed of two to three launch areas; these constructions had the form of simple concrete platform of 20 meters to 11 meters are difficult to identify. Of 6,500 units produced by the German V2, 3,170 were dropped on targets:

- 1,664 on Belgium (1,610 of Antwerp, 27 of Lüttich, 13 in Hasselt, 9 in Tournai, 3 of Mons, 2 of Dienst).
- 1,403 on England (1359 London, 43 in Norwich, Ipswich 1).
- 73 on France (25 of Lille, 19 in Paris, 19 in Tourcoing, 6 in Arras, 4 of Cambrai).
- 19 on Holland (Maastricht).
- 11 on Germany (goal the Remagen bridge over the Rhine, taken intact from American Truppo in 1945).

The V2, after the war, became the starting point for the realization of all the great families of ballistic missiles developed in the USSR, Britain, France and the USA, where von Braun, despite its "discussed" the Nazi past, he became the father of the American space program.

V2 and submarines

In order to launch the V2 on the American territory it was expected to address the Kriegsmarine, but it was not so simple after all because the missile A-4 / V2 was an Army program. But the Oberkommando wanted this solution and in December 1944 passed all resistance of the German Armed Forces and the 11th of that month constituted in Peenemunde the Study Committee to make a very difficult project to carry and launch from the sea an A-4 missile, it was already difficult and dangerous to pull from the ground under standard conditions. They became interested in the project Dr. Dikmann of Vulcan shipyards, Ing. Riedel, Gen. Rosmann and the group was called Elektro Werke Mechanishe Karlshagen. At the end of the design he arrived in a container in the shape of heavy submarine 500 tons and 45 meters long. With cruciform control surfaces and openable ogive into two sections at the time of need, had inside the missile in the front, there was then under the ethyl alcohol tank and under still, liquid oxygen, hydrogen peroxide, including pumps of trim and ballast tanks. Everything was controlled cable, the same that made the container driven by submarine. For the launch of the system was to be vertical, with a maximum inclination of 1.5 degrees; the missile was not possible to take already loaded and ready to launch, was already a step forward that there was a ready tested. Prepared the container, the staff left the 'floating ramp' with a sleeve, and then the missile at launch breaking of the frangible side plates for the exhaust gases. The container was not to be missed: every U-boat, maybe the type Type XXI or IX, was to bring the two tow and pull of 300 km, but after the launch of the containers could be ballasted and towed to the base or assigned to refuel submarines thereby making it possible to use the U-Boot in tasks 'normal'.

Since then, the Vulkan shipyard in Szczecin were quick to deliver the prototype and to launch mass production. The first and only launch was made after March 25, the day of delivery, in the Baltic Sea, in the vicinity of Peenemunde. It seems that it was a success, and was scheduled to build 60 launchers which would allow to bring V2 500 per month to the US. This would require the use of each pitcher at least twice a week, and 250 to 500 missions per month to the US. Considering the losses of German submarines, it is unlikely that these results could also have only be approached. Moreover, the campaign of far simpler V1 shooting was scheduled in 3,000 weapons a day, when the maximum was 316. It was all very ambitious. In fact, the problems would have been phenomenal: navigate with one or two containers of the kind in the Atlantic, in emerging or dipping (the compensation of these speakers 'wire-guided submarines' also allowed the motion under water) would be an 'difficult feat of his own, even without considering the technical problems of V2. In stormy conditions would be difficult to achieve the conditions for precise launch, since already from the ground, precisely knowing where you flushed, the error was a few km; 300 km and in the sea there was no way with absolute precision to know your location. All this then did not consider that the United States in 1945 were dangerous enough for the U-boats even when it came to operate in Europe. A slow and difficult sailing to New York would have to put in mind their efforts dall'USN. Stop hour stop in front of the American coast was ultimately extremely dangerous, i had long since passed time 'easy' early 1942. The difference between this solution, albeit technically acceptable, and what was accomplished then is indicative, just think of the submarines 'Golf' type and 'Hotel' Russian with missiles derived from V2. But these submarines had integrated missiles inside them, in large and stable platforms. Perhaps for the V2 would be very useful, rather, the large submarines dimensions such as I-401 Japanese, more than sufficient for the purpose.

Certainly, if one of these actions was successful, it would be a propaganda remarkable coup importance for Germany. But in March 1945 the Americans were passing the Rhine and the Third Reich had only weeks to live, while the scarce fuel for every branch of the Armed Forces. Eventually, if Germany had been able to launch a nuclear V2, the thing could have any influence on the destiny of the nation. Rather, it is hard to understand why the much more simple V1 was not taken into account for the launch of a large submarine. This after all was done, after the war, with an American program that concerned the Loon, a copy of V1, which were then developed up to the powerful missile Regulus I and II (supersonic). Just think of the submarines with various seaplanes and bulky related accommodations. However it does not seem that the V1 has ever been considered, perhaps because of their vulnerability, as sublanciate weapons.

Operation Backfire

If the Americans had put his hands on V2 and other advanced technologies with the 'Paperclip' project, which began July 19, 1945 with the appointment of a number of German technicians, the British who suffered more than anyone else rocket attacks were very quick to make the same and, moreover, preceded the Americans, whose first launch of a V2 White Sands on April 16, 1946 was above all a failure. Instead the British, with considerable cunning and a good dose of luck, they were able to launch as many as 3 missiles from Cuxhaven. This despite the fact that on May 30 many as 14 tons of German documents were brought from Antwerp in the United States, were the treasure retrieved in a mine Dörnten, which however remained very briefly. Along with these they took away roughly the equivalent of 400 rail wagons with enough to assemble about 100 V2. But between the Soviets and the Americans, in the race to grab what was left of German technology and technical and related scientists, the third competitor could enjoy it, at least for the moment. The 21st Army Group staff landmarks in the Netherlands and West Germany to rebuild a launch battery V2 missiles, and before May 2, 1945 von Braun will hand over to the Americans, the English had begun, thanks to the idea of commander JCBernard. Operation Backfire, so named because of the view of Colonel Carter, managed already by May 20 to find 30/2 to set up a real launch units. The British thought they soon have thirty missiles, but did not know that the V2 were 'perishable' materials that were launched within a week to not end up with the internal components out of action for a minimum of moisture or other problems caused by 'environment.

Indeed, it was better if they threw within three days to reduce malfunctions in only 4% instead of 20 as initially happened against Britain. Eventually it was decided that Cuxhaven was suitable for the experimental launch of these weapons, to reduce in-range 240 km instead of 320 in order not to hit Denmark. But on May 26 it was realized that the V2 officially found were not in conditions which will ensure the campaign of shots expected, with great scorn of the English who had this idea. Indeed, the era of missiles guaranteed for ten years without maintenance (or almost) and ICBM capable of staying on alert for consecutive years, was far. The surviving factories were mostly in the East to rescue them from the Allied bombs and this means that despite the move to the South made towards the end of the war, were now in Soviet hands.

He tried for six weeks all the small companies that were subcontractors of the 30,000 members of the V2, in spite of everything because there were not even enough manuals and those present disagreed with each other, given that the production lots of the V2 were not necessarily compatible.

Despite all the difficulties, the end came 400 trucks and 640 tons of tools and construction drawings. Despite all the difficulties the Germans, marveling at the Allies, had executed shots until March 1945, but now there was no way to have sufficient subsystems to assemble some V2.

Many components, such as graphite blades for jet deflector had been sabotaged, even the last V2 Peenemunde was blown up on its ramp 27 February 1945, when von Braun will set foot for the last time. But in the end there were in Cuxhaven 2,500 British and nearly 4,000 Germans, including persons of the von Braun team. You had to get a lot of things, he had to trust the Germans to whose head was put on with. Weber; is built workshop 90 meters long and finally found a plant for the production of liquid oxygen, of which served 5 tons for the launch of a V2, but in reality 9 were needed to compensate for losses.

There was a need of pure alcohol at least 93%, which came from Nordhausen, and so on. On October 2, were well 12

V2 discoveries including 8 almost in perfect condition. Now really they were assembled all the 'pieces'. With few resources, thus beating the Americans and the Soviets, the British passed the first pitches of the postwar V2, of which 314 experimental and 3,600 operative had been used in the war.

He tried to start the V2 already on October 2, but nothing happened. But on October 3, at 14:43, the V2 really left. She arched in the sky and in just 4 minutes and 50 seconds came to hit a point with a gap of 2.4 kilometers to the left and short of 1.6 km, still better than a bullet equivalent artillery range. Then it was the turn of a V2 on October 4, but only traveled 24 km in 35 seconds and finally 15 October 1945 another missile was pulled, this time with a large crowd of guests Allies, and for the relief of the English, and despite a wind of less than 43 km / h the launch worked perfectly. The mission was completed as of October 20, when the staff was released, but only twenty agreed to continue working with the British. So this sort of 'circus' was broken up without further consequences, but a 40-minute documentary, 5 volumes delivered in January 1947 to the War Office, and various materials put in museums. The British had no other consequences. They paid much less the Americans and the Soviets, and perhaps even that counted.

The missile had English despite this absence of German contribution also a very interesting development, with original and unrelated projects from what was produced in the rest of the world. But he departed late, even by that, although they were the first to operate a V2 after the war, did not receive long-lasting consequences for their technology: an impromptu and resounding success, which, however, in the impoverished Britain never to be heard or not he would realize.

V2 in the USSR

The Soviets entered Peenemunde May 5, 1945, putting his hands on the 'Holy Grail' of advanced research of the time. But not very interesting find, when the center, defended to the last by the SS, was now stripped of many of its resources, such as radar Wurzuburg Riese, the wind tunnel of Mach 4.4 supersonic built by Rudolph Hermman (supply in Bavaria, Kochel). The test beds were almost all damaged, including those for Wasserfall missiles and for smaller SAM Taifun type. The school I was still present, was that to which he was attached in the spring the rocket motor 25 tons of thrust, then brought to 27 although 1.3 'eaten' by directional graphite panels when directed 20 degrees. It was not only for the advance of the Soviets that we moved to the South of Germany, but also for fear of other attacks such as that on 17-18 August 1943 the RAF, dear paid in truth, but which destroyed a lot of infrastructure, killing 735 people including more than 600 prisoners of war were reduced to forced laborers. Also died occasion Dr. Thiel, ie the engine designer Wasserfall C-1 and A-4 (V2). Not only that, it was also the designer of a monstrous engine to an intercontinental ballistic missile called A-9 or A-10. In fact the same bank 1 was capable of withstanding more than 200 tons of thrust and this engine arrived, at least although the design to 180. It was difficult putting all the pieces in place now. For example, V2 were constructed on the basis of 6,450 construction drawings, they had 30,000 different components, but many machines had been brought in 111,000 m2 underground factory in Thuringia 260 km away. The test beds were also needed for the V2 engines, which were to prove to function properly at least 65 seconds, served by a plant producing something like 115 kg of liquid oxygen per minute. But of all this there remained a lot, as well as technicians 4,325 and 760 employees still present in February, with great scorn of the Col Vavilov who led the troops who arrived at Peenemunde. The fact is that von Braun had decided to opt for moving westward and the Germans did not want to leave at Peenemunde valuable materials and men, starting the migration for Thuringia February 17, 1945, with a train of 525 people. In short, the Soviets were initially empty-handed. Americans instead found some 250 V2 at Mittelwerk. But the area was assigned to the USSR, for which they should have been 'his'. Instead the Americans in nine days did disappear 640 tons of materials in 300 railway wagons including 510,101 drawings and 3,500 relations. May 2, von Braun was in Bavaria with its best technicians and their families, ready to surrender to the Americans. Ninety of them actually went to France and became the backbone of the French missile until all'Ariane 4. But it was not all lost because of the 2000 V2 available at the end of March 1945, about half were in areas that were under German control Soviet. 515 were sent immediately to the USSR, but there were so many problems in reliability, which had to be virtually rebuilt. No wonder because the engines had already subsystems 500 and 1,800 elements, and especially the economy with which the V2 were built was that having to launch a real expiration date: within the seven days of completion. By way of valves, gyroscopes, electrical resistances, so that up to 20% of V2 delivered to the departments they had to be returned for rework to MITTELWERK, or to be used as spare parts for new ones. What's more the V2 captured usually were sabotaged, for example, gyroscopes and the graphite jet deflectors, finally the rust was a further problem in those months of storage. The Soviets reached the underground base of Nordhausen only July 5, again finding it ransacked by the Americans.

If only the productive machinery were not lacking, because the pace of construction had reached 500 units per month in January, but operating missiles there was almost nothing usable. Toakaev, a leading expert of Russian missile, was quite depressed even though he thought to organize in Germany a working group to rebuild the V2 with a lot of forced or left volunteers German engineers. Now the problem was that in the West there were already many 'customers' of the German technology. The last V2 was pulled over London until after March 28, 1945, to October but three English V2 were pulled from Cuxhaven just to assess the ballistic. In truth there was little to measure because it in 200 days of bombing had rained down on London 3065 V2, with an error on the 2.5% target (which incidentally means about 7 km to the maximum range). Especially the reliability had proved exceptional, with over 90% of successful launches, though often the missiles exploded in the back with the atmosphere despite all the attempts to insulate well tested. It took hard work, however, for the Soviets, and October 18, 1947, over 2 years later, finally drew a V2 from Volgograd and thanks only to the 'Collective' 'German specialists, volunteers or not to be. The improved version, the R-1, waited until 18 October 1948. Among the protagonists of the birth of Soviet missile it was also col. Valentin Glunsko Korolev (survived the 'purges' that hit him, but rehabilitated thanks to the KGB who appreciated his talents as a designer), and who spoke fluent German. It was a great advantage, because it did not have to wait for the translation of documents, and could speak or directly interrogate the scientists and the German engineers. Nor has it been so easy, with Stalin that he wanted the restoration of the drawings and the creation of a production line in Germany. Thus, under the so-veiled threat not to end up in a gulag, the three Soviets went to work setting up the Rabe in Berlin, in the employ of gen.

Kutsentsov. Needed qualified people to the cloning of the V2 program and among them was certainly the best helmu Grottrup, electronics expert and guidance systems, and paid monthly with 5,000 marks if he had accepted the post, four times what took von Braun with the Americans . And, in fact, there was real hope that these could change his jacket, which would have even changed history. But it did not happen because the Soviets hoped. This scientist also was very good also in the working structure 'pyramid' experienced in Peenemunde, with a final referent and many superspecialists to make the components. That was how von Braun showed up to the Americans, with 118 technicians and the director of Kurt Debus launches.

Before long Grottrup replaced the first non excelled Director Dr. Rosemplenter to Rabe and bringing dint of engagements staff from 30 to 5,000 in just one year. In the end, 30 new V2 were sent in Russia, and many centers were created for specialized tasks, such as the Werk II for the V2 engines. Finally the Soviet order for an experimental train from 80-100 wagons to run the test launch of V2, although officially it was just a 'Mobile meteorological train'. There will, however, never launches V2 from Germany. A Lehesten continued testing, where Glushko had produced already in September a high power motor. Then in the summer of 1946 began technical development required for a longer range. The secrecy of the work was such that for years even the construction of the R-7 missile (SS-6) remained uncertain, so much so that even in the late 50's were thought to be equipped with only a 5-R-14 engines of 120 tons of thrust , never existed engines in that form. Among the changes it was to make the detachable warhead with explosive bolts to increase the range, a kind of two-stage missile, in fact they were old ideas for missiles already experienced towards the end of the war, with such features.

The fact is, 13 May 1946 Stalin had given birth to the State Commission for the study of long-range rockets or PKRDD. This was readily defined various OKB, as the OKB-456 MAP of Glushko, for rocket motors, and various institutions such as the NII-88 MW for ballistic rockets Korolev, the NII-885 MPSS for guidance systems and others including the Council of Designers, bringing together the various driving branches, propulsion and launch systems. Korolev would have then gone into in his OKB, since 1954 became the OKB-1, all the experiences and the progress of the other centers and OKB. There were also workshops Zadov 88 and 456, which were promptly sent the missiles and components products to Zentralwerke and its German subsidiaries; thus the work of 7,000 employees in East Germany was 'shot' to the Soviets, to mislead Americans about the origin of this progress. The first rockets were improved with the R-1 powertrain improved slightly, known as SS-1 Scunner for NATO, and the R-2, which would have had twice the original output, known as SS-2 Sibling. It goes without saying that at this point, to enhance missiles however expensive and inaccurate, it was necessary to have an atomic warhead. But even this was coming. Meanwhile, Stalin wanted to concentrate all the work in the Soviet territory and on October 22 he was ordained to 2,500 Germans, including Grottrup, leaving Germany (he who in order not to leave it had accepted the Soviet engagement) and find themselves routed in multiple locations and factories . but in the end they found themselves mostly grouped Gorodomljia. Among their tasks there were bizarre, how to verify the possibility of a 'antipolare' bomber as suggested by Sanders, with an engine of 100 tons thrust that had been partially realized during the war. A sort of space shuttle before its time, which was to go into orbit and then run it on enemy territory bombings. Thanks to them also were born enhanced versions of the A-4 / V2 engines: the RD-

100, with more divergent discharge to increase the output thrust RD-101 with pressure greater than 40% and used for R -2, the RD-103 with 60% of the increased discharge pressure and used for the R-5 or SS-3 Shyster, from 1,200 km away, while the RD-102 was an intermediate step that was not realized. They were then studied other types of weapons, such as the G-1 600-km-range, called R-4 or R-10 by the Soviets, who had self-supporting tanks (that is pressurized to 2 atmospheres, which made the structure of the lighter missile , albeit with increase in thickness from 1.5 to 4 mm), so that the radius was then extended to 810 km, while the guidance systems were moved under the tanks. The head was covered in wood but made nonflammable with an appropriate chemical process. He remained on paper, but it was an interesting guy. In 1947 it was formed the first Soviet cosmodrome, called Volgograd Station, which preceded approximately eight years Baikonur. Many of the facilities were on two German trains, the FMS-1 and 2, which has been talked about before. Grottrup and other technicians were sent there, and on October 18, at 10.47 could run the launch of missiles with a V2 T (telemetry) that was launched in more than 206 km, although the second launch, two days later, he saw the 'weapon stop at 152 m altitude and then fell, prompting accusations of sabotage. Followed by other tests and then the Germans departed for Gorodomljia. In 1948 he started the project of a missile by 2,500 km and 1,000-kg warhead, which was called G-2 by the Germans and R-12 or R-6 by the Soviets. There was need for a new project and with engines of 100 tons of thrust. The project was interesting, but was overcome by the G-4 to 3000 km and 3 tons of thrust, required 9 April 1949 by the Minister Ustinov. The reason was the possibility of transporting the Soviet atomic throughout Europe, and, in fact, on August 29 of that year the first 'atomic' was blasted. So this missile was studied but even that had a long life; It provided for a single high-stage 23,65 meters with a base diameter of 2.74, a weight of 70 tons full load, and just 6.160 vacuum, with an engine of 101 tons thrust. A cylinder head protected by 400 kg of steel and (internally) wood, engine 60 atmospheres of pressure, without the gas generator but with power turbine with the combustion gases. The September 21, 1949 was pulled the first R-2 with engine RD-101 37 tons. The Soviets took meanwhile designs and the material produced by the Germans, who finally hoped to do something more that consultants to increase the fame of local scientists, as Korolev. There were also other projects, such as R-3 4,000 km range, and then to be improved as the R-3A, ancestor R-7 intercontinental. This was the work of Glunshko, with an engine of 7,000 kgs and conical nozzles replaced by more divergent complexes, who made about 3% of the thrust. Other ideas were taken up perhaps by engines from 8,000 kgs of Wasserfall anti-aircraft. Finally were designed rockets vernieri 3,000 kgs, which were an alternative to the far more complex nozzle structure gimbal. Finally the Germans, from March 21, 1951 al 30 November 1953 were sent back to Germany, after they had in fact helped to give birth to a class of Soviet technicians who had acted as instructors. Meanwhile it was launched the R-5 missile was the extreme evolution of the V2 technology. In the R-5M version, this weapon of 20.74 meters came to 1,200 kilometers and could strike with a small nuclear warhead, which made him rather formidable to Westerners. It was produced in small series in 1956, and was the counterpart, but with much greater range, American Redstone, well as it proceeds from the V2 technology. Finally, the 'children' of Soviet rockets V2 and their technicians were converted into weapons geophysical or atmospheric reconnaissance launches high altitude. Bombs were made as early as 1949, and designated with V1 as a basic reference, and various sub-versions, up to 18 meters high, with scientific equipment; already the first arrived at 110 km May 24, 1949. In 1955 a V-1E lifted to 100km a load of 1.8 tons, including dogs, rabbits, mice. Then it was the turn of the R-2 converted to V2 (certainly not the 'original'), always with side containers that had equipment from dropping by parachute or warheads equipped with special air brakes. One of them, 16 May 1957, came to 200 km with filming systems and chemical analysis apparatus. The dogs were launched in Mass: at least 100 pairs in 1955-60 and R-5 rocket used since 1957, he led to impressive 480 km above its load of 1,350 kg and two dogs. Was higher than the others, well 23,74 meters.

In short, the Soviets realized their first generation of ballistic missiles through the efforts and contributions of the various Peenemundiani, but he never attributed any merit, which did not fail to upset the German scientists. In 1958 Grottrup like this to the German DGRR (a society for space flight) a memorial telling the work done for years in the Soviet Union, at least to restore the historical truth.

V2 and the birth of the French rocketry

It was France that had the dubious honor of finding themselves targeted by the first A-4 ballistic missiles that have ever been launched into war. Penguin was the operation, which had as commander Hans Krammler. There were three battalions well with 6,300 soldiers and 1,600 vehicles, with 485 Battalion in North, South and in the 836 ° and 444 ° of the SS. The objective was mainly London but was later also added Paris, released in late August. It tried to pull two V2 September 6, but did not work for defects in the ignition systems or power (in any case it would not know to take off), but the September 8 (apparently at 8:34, after 4 minutes flight) a missile of 444 ° was successful albeit pulled by 290 km. Paris still was not particularly ill-treated, given that at most he throws for 22 V2, which mistook the target even of 70 km. Perhaps there was a willingness to strike, while some did not fail to London and Antwerp, while centered 350 devices, starting from the same day with a shot close to Waterloo Station due to the activity of the 485th Battalion. Initially the British did believe that it was a gas leak, but then had to admit that there were weapons inintercettabili who were in their capital. Moureu Henry, director of the State Laboratory of research in Paris soon realized that these weapons were the future and France could not stay out of it. The Air Ministry felt the same way and from 9 May 1945 gave him the mandate to recover everything possible, together with the technical J.J. Barré who had tested the EA in 1941, the first endoreattore in French liquid propellants, from about 1,000 kgs, 17 March of that year. They wanted to find at least a dozen V1 and V2; the first were actually granted by the Anglo-Americans, so that the Nord Aviation used them as a basis for aerobersaglio CT-10, which was basically a clone them with pulsogetto

Arsenal. But for V2 things he got less well, and the only thing that looked like the claim to have the V2 was to rummage in Cuxhaven, where the British had very swiftly put to test, even without subsequent outcomes, V2. But there were certainly not many materials used and the French had to make do with what little they were able to scrape together, especially with the help of the DEFA (Studies and Production Armaments), which among other things would give the body early DEFA cannon same name by 30 mm, made by German technology revolver guns. The CEPA was born on November 4, 1945, which is the study center-propelled weapons. Its tasks were twofold: to rebuild the advanced German weapons, and improve them in range and payload. Technicians were found in Cuxhaven and Trauen for a total of 90 hired to May 15, 1946. On May 17, was proposed the construction of a center that later became the seat of the SEP, the manufacturer of the Ariane, Vernon, a town in Normandy . The German technicians were initially used in two groups to study the guidance systems and the engines, but there was also a small detachment to make engines for tanks of 1,000 hp being these technicians Maybach. Among the innovations studied was that of a gas generator already patented in 1942 by Ing. Bringer, who was then working with Thiel. It was a system in which the propellant burning at 3,000 degrees in a combustion chamber, which temperature was then reduced to 600 degrees with distilled water, which was used to pressurize the tanks with the gases produced by eliminating the large and heavy turbopumps. This alone was enough to increase the range to 550 km of a V2, but you also wanted an engine of 40 tons of thrust. Meanwhile, the gas generator of this type, in many variations, will be used until the rocket Ariane 4. Then the French, as they tried to rebuild the V2 in the workshops of Poteaux, thought to various new projects such as a ballistic missile to 100 km, PARCA radio-SAM missile, a rocket probe, a strategic rocket called Eole. Meanwhile V2 put together in the workshops of Poteaux, despite all efforts would not hear of materializing. Only one of the thirty foreseen was completed in late 1947, and it was thought that we would not have arrived at the total expected before 1952. An old missile over ten years, however, did not represent the future, and so it was decided the planned project with the A9 engine to nitric acid and diesel fuel, combined with the entirely French EA 1946 Project engineer Barré, but failed two launches in 1952 and ended miserably. Not even the Super V2 or A9 had better luck, being abandoned. But to technical Bringer he was told to continue to develop the gas generator. He was also interested in small rockets to nitric acid and kerosene, a legacy of the Wasserfall engine. In any case, in 1948 the project of the Super V2 was canceled, but at least the Germans technicians Vernon began to produce rocket-probe of excellent features, up to the launch of satellite systems. The first was the Veronique, like a small V2, cost only $ 10,000, 6.5 meters long, 55 cm diameter, with 710 kg of nitric acid and diesel engine from 4,000 kgs to 31.5 sec, total weight up to 1,435 kg. Was devoid of gyroscopes, but to stabilize resorted to 4 balanced voltage cables of 4 horizontal bars, arranged to break away at 60 meters, motor with regenerative cooling, and variable portion. Depending on the version, it passed 70 km well 200. He went into production in 1952 and they were launched no less than 66 until 1968, the last to inaugurate the Kaurou space base in French Guyana. Years passed and he tried to launch a European program for carriers Europe, but its subsystems were useful and Bringer improved before Veronique and then devoted himself to the big Vesta, 14,400 kg of thrust, weight of 5,400 kg and an option to place well 500 kg to 600 km altitude load. Meanwhile all'ONERA of Chatillon, the French were able to develop the sounding rocket LEX weighing just 76 kilograms but was taking an initial boost of about 1,000 kg, which then decayed in 30-35 seconds at about 200. But after 8 successful launch was abandoned despite having an interesting engine with coal and nitromethane (ie a solid-liquid system). In 1962 came the carriers for even satellites in Europe. It took the space-based ballistic missile launchers English Blue Streak, yet December 18, 1961 was launched the plan for the pitcher Diamant and formed the CNES or the Space Research Centre. Pitchers Europe, despite the London Agreement of 23 March 1962 signed by seven nations, came to nothing, but then gave way to the experience very useful for future ESA space agency. Meanwhile, in France the technicians had assembled the engine system Verix from 30 tons, used for the rocket Emeraude, but especially in November 1965 was launched the Diamant, well 18.9 meters high with two stages, consisting of a Emeraude and by a Topaze ; Finally there was a small Rubis with a load of 41 kg with Asterix satellite, but after a while he stopped sending signals. Followed by other satellites, the Diapason of 17 February 1966 and 8 February 1967. They were Diadema launches performed from Algeria, from Hammaguir polygon, but after that was closed and all the launches were continued in Kourou, beginning with two DIAL satellites and People, on the rocket Diamant B from 23.5 meters and 160 kg payload. The rocket was used until 1973 gradually improved, including the engine Valois from 40 tons of thrust, which was really the last of the possible evolutionary degrees of dell'A.9 Bringer Project, and so carried a load of 200 kg for low orbit of 300 km, while the launch mass was 27.5 tons. Only three launches, all by 1975. Finally came the Viking for the Ariane rockets.

Bringer was still, with the last ten Germans of Vernon and many French now well educated in the field, to turn to the bench engine Viking 1 to 55 tons that was destined to rocket Europa 3, what else would not have been if not the 'Ariane. It's amazing, but this engine was based conceptually on a functional type from 1,000 kgs of 1942, a small prototype. The engine cooling system was simplified with a pump for the water used to cool the gases and the motor generator used the same main propellants. It was far simpler the equally powerful American Rocketdyne S.3 with cooling system and regenerative structures in general more complex. Viking at The 1971 will follow the Viking II by 73.5 tons. In the end, the success of the Ariane rocket was full and the motor Viking has been replaced only by the Vulcain with hydrogen and liquid oxygen. Eng. Karl-Heinz Bringer he retired in 1976, after 30 years of service with the experimental center of Vernon, and died January 2, 1999 at age 90. One of the last among the 500 engineers Peenemunde, that for decades, in the aerospace world exerted a great design and conceptual influence. People able to design valid in 1942 after 50 years systems (one could also speak of Soviet developments such as those of scud missiles, for example), and that to all effects have continued to do, despite the black shadow of the program A-4 / V2, which von Braun basically considered a 'necessary evil' to continue the space program on their careers. As the same von Braun, gradually fell into oblivion after the progressive lack of interest in space missions, others have sought in their professional lives to progress in the use of space propulsion, hoping maybe one day see realized the most important mission conceived by their leader, a manned space mission to Mars, already envisaged in 1952 by von Braun. They could well define idealists in their striving towards such research, although often fattisi manipulated by the military and the politicians.

94

Technical features

Dimensions and weights

- Weight: 13,500 kg
- Diameter: 1.65 meters
- Height: 14.00 meters
- Wingspan: 3.56 meters
- Guide system: radio
- Copies: 5,200
  - Up to September 15, 1944: 1,900
  - September 15 to October 29, 1944: 900
  - October 29 to November 24, 1944: 600
  - November 24 to January 15, 1945: 1,100
  - January 15 to February 15, 1945: 700

Performance

- Range: 320-360 km
- Maximum speed: 5760 km / h
- Propellant: 3,810 kg of ethanol (75%) and water (25%) and 4,910 kg of liquid oxygen.
- Explosive: TNT and ammonium nitrate (1.000 kg)
- explosion When the V-2 was capable of causing a crater 20 meters wide and 8 meters deep, with the expulsion of about 3,000 tons of material in the air.

Wasserfall

The Wasserfall was a great German anti-aircraft missile World War II, like the others in its class did not have time to go into service but it was a weapon impressive, like the SA-2, with a range of 48 km even calculated. His projects were a model for the US missile Hermes-A1 and the Soviet research program known under the name R-101. The Wasserfall was essentially an antiaircraft development of V2 rocket, keeping the same shape and the same design. Since it was to reach only the flight altitude of the big Allied bombers, it was reduced by about a quarter of the size compared to V2 rockets; 7.85 meters long, weighed 3,700 kg, had a range of 25 km and a top speed of 770 meters per second. Unlike their progenitors, the Wasserfall were designed to launch which could be delayed for periods exceeding one month and over, for this reason, the liquid oxygen, excessively volatile, it was not appropriate for the purpose. Consequently was designed a new engine designed by the Walter Thiel, based on Visol (vinyl ether esobutile) and on RFNA, consisting of 84% nitric acid, from 13% of dinitrogen trioxide and from 1-2% water . This hypergolic propellant was pushed into the combustion chamber together with nitrogen released from a separate tank. Originally the head was 100 kg, but subsequently was replaced with a 306 kg on the basis of a liquid explosive. The idea was to create a large explosive effect in the middle of the enemy bomber formation that would, in theory, could bring down several aircraft with a single launched missile, with an operator that would detonate the warhead by remote control. The guidance system was based on a radio control of manual command to line of sight type, against diurnal objectives, while for night launches the use of this rocket was much more complex due to the poor visibility of both the rocket that same lens.

With a manual command to line of sight missile, the operator had to keep an eye on both the missile and the objective the same time and guide the missile to the target.

"Wasserfall" exhibited at the National Museum of the US Air Force.

Usually the missile was being maneuvered with a joystick; the manual command to line of sight required a workout and considerable practice to be mastered, so the accuracy achieved by manual command to line of sight missile is hard to picture, since it was highly dependent on operator skill. To overcome this problem was designed a new help system denominated in Rheinland code which, however, remained at the stage of development. The guidance system Rheinland would have to make use of a transponder place within the rocket in flight and for the localization of a radar to keep track of the target.

The V3

The V3 Hochdruckpumpe (or the high-pressure pump) was a prototype super-cannon made by Germany during the latter stages of World War II. V3 is the acronym for Vergeltungswaffe 3 ("weapon of reprisal 3" from the German), on the idea of Joseph Goebbels to change its name to some weapons for propaganda purposes. The cannon, which measured 140 meters in length, was capable of firing grenades up to 140 kg with a range of about 165 kilometers, from Mimoyecques near Calais on the French coast, as far as London. The main idea was to use gunpowder to provide the necessary thrust so that the bullet could get out of the barrel of the cannon with the speed necessary to reach the goal. The push was done gradually, by exploding grenades at the side of the barrel. It was therefore a fairly economical solution. The original program consisted of twenty-five of these weapons, in Marquise-Mimoyecques between Calais and Boulogne, which, after completion of the design phase, they had to launch 200 grenades per hour (but after making a Hillersleben tests in autumn 1943 and Miedzyzdroje in January 1944, it was decided that it could increase the rate of fire of 50%). A prototype of 20 mm was developed in a test site in Misdroy (islet north of Poland), and the success was demonstrated in April-May of 1943. It was then dug a deep tunnel in the rock thirty meters and protected by a dome the thickness of 5.2 meters. Were dug in the ground gypsum (marl, typical of the area) a series of inclined at approximately 45 °, connected by a checkerboard of horizontal tunnel tunnel, the upper ones which open in the rail tunnel of almost 2 kilometers and those lower than the base of the inclined tunnel, to a depth of about 60 meters, positioned below the ground water with the related sealing problems. From the beginning, the Germans realized that the mechanism had drawbacks, such as the collapse in some parts of the barrel, and the instability of the projectile when it exceeded the speed of 1,100 m / s. Minister of Armaments Albert Speer was convinced, however, that a better gauge of the projectile could overcome this. In reality, according to the Luxembourg museum, going to change the angle between the joints, the volume of the secondary chambers, the distance that elapsed between them, the amount of gunpowder and the initial speed of the projectile, you could get to sagging very more dilated in time, or from a value of 10 after launch to about 10,000.

The weapon was designed by the company Röchling Eisen - und Stahlwerke Leipzig, who presented the idea to Speer that, curiously, ordered a feasibility study to the firm Saar Rochling. The gun had a barrel length of 130 meters, and a capacity to shoot grenades of 140 kg even at 165 km away (actually in testing never reached such a distance). The idea of the gun type can be traced back to Baron Von Guido Pirquet, who studied the system of lateral slots to electrically activated in sequence angle to provide additional acceleration to the grenade during its passage inside the weapon.

This allowed an output speed of over 1,500 m / s. The maximum speed of theoretical output was to reach 1,700 m/s at an angle of 39° cannon, during the tests, however, I never exceeded 1.170 m/s (with the gun tube of 15 cm FH18 not went beyond 935 m/s). At these speeds the projectiles were not very stable, so it was decided to equip them with small fins of 2.5 cm radially sull'affusto for stability (only twenty years after the Canadians resumed the idea in the series of Martlet). Then immediately they began the excavation of the tunnels, which are necessary for the construction of the imposing cannon in the north coast of France, going to then form the third weapon of terror after the V-1 and V-2.

Prototype of V3 with inclined combustion chambers of 90 °.

The French site plan foresaw the inclined side of combustion chambers of a certain angle (45 °) and placed at a distance of 3.65 meters from each other.

Section of V3 with inclined combustion chambers of 45 °.

At its construction they were dedicated many Slavic workers, but the French resistance, given the initial construction efforts, immediately warned the allies, who regularly, only two months later, the bombing began. The massive protective bubble, however, played a great role, resisted even the Tallboy bombs from 5.4 tons. Eventually, July 6, 1944, the dome gave way, however, screwed by three bombs that failed to runs to the end the tunnel. The disaster was complete: the bottom of the base, where the prisoners were kept about 800 forced laborers during the bombing, which filled with water by killing them all. Despite the success ally, the Americans with Aphrodite project continued until the month of August 1944 to bomb the coastal bunkers using the B-17 radio-guided, but then suspended the operation for the few achievements and the many accidents occurred, as well as to having to mobilize the main effort of the bombers on the regions of Germany. In one such incident, 12 August 1944, in England as he was flying toward Mimoyecques, died Joseph Kennedy Jr., older brother of the future president. Allied advance before the base was abandoned. In 1945 it was widely dinamitata by the British genius to avoid a possible anti-English usage (united Europe was still far and involved the city demolition all German bases in the north of France).

Do not know, therefore, the actual potential of this weapon, considering that very few shots were fired, which could still be triggered. An abridged version of the cannon was used against the city of Luxembourg, who has been released in September 1944. The first shots were fired Dec. 30, 1944 for a total of 183 strokes, up to February 22, 1945, with 44 confirmed facilities in ' urban area. The weapon did not prove very effective: the joints shots sign caused 10 dead and 35 wounded. The V3 project therefore concerned the realization of a new conception supercannon, called Hochdruckpumpe ("high-pressure pump"), able to bomb London from Calais. The initial idea was by engineer August Conders, who proposed the creation of a cannon in which were detonated successively more charges, so as to impart to the projectile an extremely high initial velocity and thus achieve thrown otherwise unthinkable. The project provided that along the barrel of the weapon, extremely long, were placed in succession, to both sides, of various solid propellant charges for rockets, each placed in a lateral appendix of the barrel itself (the appearance resulting earned weapon the name to "Tausendfüßler" code, centipedes); not being the rifled barrel, the bullet would have been firmly maintained by ailerons. Being the very long barrel, the weapon would be housed in underground sites with the barrel supported by the land itself. The first prototypes of the weapon gave very disappointing results: besides the fact that the initial velocity of the projectile provided was much lower than expected, the tests conducted at Misdroy, on the Baltic island of Wolin, revealed the existence of serious problems with the system shutter and with the conception of the projectiles. With the commitment of companies like Krupp and Skoda these flaws were partially resolved and in May 1944 were carried out some tests with a barrel length of about 150 meters, during which they were joined thrown 80-90 km; But the cannon exploded, putting an end to attempts. In the meantime he had begun the construction of a new site to Mimoyecques, at Calais, that in the original intention was to include 50 weapons divided into two complex compounds from 5 slots for 5 guns each, connected by underground complexes; in reality the constraints due to the performance of the conflict forced to drastically downsize the initial project. Construction began in September 1944 by the Organisation Todt, who was building near also launch sites for V1 and V2; But the allied air reconnaissance revealed the work and various air strikes began to target the site. These bombings had little effect, because the slots had been protected by a concrete dome 5.2 meters thick, with a steel door opening; but July 6, 1944 a new bombardment was conducted with the use of high-penetration bombs, the so-called "Tallboy", which caused the destruction of an accommodation and serious damage to the site underground tunnel, leading to the abandonment of the construction. In fact the history of the V3 project was not over: the SS General Hans Kammler took control of the project and ordered the construction of two smaller weapons, with cane 50 meters, to be placed in Lampaden, near Trier, to bomb Luxembourg and the Ardennes; with the failure of the Ardennes offensive the two guns were abandoned, after firing a few shots with little effect.

V-3: The Vengeance Weapon

Nazi scientists developed the last of the V-weapons in a final effort to obliterate London

Another attempt was made in Alsace in conjunction with the Operation Nordwind for the reconquest of Alsace-Lorraine, but the offensive failed before weapons were ready. Thus ended the brief and unfortunate history of the V3 project, a failed project that never give the expected results; and it is also seen by the fate that took her remains: while the allies tried to seize as many possible examples of V2 with technical related, the V3 prototypes were tested and discarded, judged nothing more than useless scrap metal.

Fortress Mimoyecques

The Mimoyecques fortress is the name of a military underground complex of World War II constructed by the forces of Nazi Germany between 1943 and 1944. It was intended to house a battery of cannons V-3 facing London, 165 kilometers away. Originally his codenamed Wiese ("meadow") or Bauvorhaben 711 ("Construction Project 711"), it is located in the town of Landrethun-le-Nord in the Pas-de-Calais region of northern France, near the Mimoyecques fraction of about 20 km from Boulogne-sur-Mer Beach. It was built by a workforce largely German primarily of engineers and miners. The complex consists of a network of tunnels dug under a clay hill, linked to five inclined trees where they would be installed 25 cannons V3, all focused on London. The weapons were capable of firing ten explosive projectiles per minute, or 600 every hour, on the British capital, which Winston Churchill later commented would have been the most devastating attack of all. The Allies knew nothing of the V3, but identified the site as a possible launch base for V2 ballistic missiles, based on reconnaissance photographs and fragmentary intelligence from French sources. Mimoyecques was targeted by heavy bombardment by the Allied air forces by the end of 1943 onwards. The construction works have been greatly hampered, forcing the Germans to abandon work on a part of the complex. The rest was partly destroyed by the July 6, 1944 617 Squadron RAF, which used penetrating bombs "Tallboy" from 5,400 kilograms to collapse tunnels and shafts, burying hundreds of workers underground. The Germans stopped the construction work at Mimoyecques since the Allies advanced up the coast as a result of the Normandy landings. He touched the 3rd Canadian Infantry Division 5 September 1944 without finding any resistance, as the Germans withdrew from the

105

area a few days earlier. The complex was partially demolished after the war under direct orders from Churchill, and much to the annoyance of the French, who were not consulted, since it was still seen as a threat to the UK. It was subsequently reopened by private owners, first in 1969 to serve as a mushroom farm, and later as a museum in 1984. An organization of nature conservation has acquired the Mimoyecques fortress in 2010 and La Coupole, a former base missile V2 becomes a museum near Saint-Omer, taking on the management. It continues to be open to the public as a museum. In May 1943 Albert Speer, Minister of the Third Reich armaments and war production, informed Adolf Hitler of the work that was being done to produce a super-cannon capable of firing hundreds of bullets per hour over long distances. The newly developed cannon, named "Hochdruckpumpe" Code ("high pressure pump", in short HDP) and then designated as the V3, was one of Vergeltungswaffen ("retaliatory weapons") developed by Nazi Germany in the later stages the war for the Allies to attack targets. Long-range cannons were not new, such as the Paris Gun (the gun used in Paris during World War II), but the high pressure detonations used to fire bullets from earlier such weapons were. In 1942, August Coenders, inspired by previous designs of multi-chamber cannons, suggested that a gradual acceleration of the projectile by a series of small charges distributed on the length of the barrel could be the solution to the problem of the design of the guns at very long range. Coenders proposed the use of electrically activated charge to eliminate the premature ignition problem encountered controlled charges from previous cannons to multiple rooms. The HDP would have had a smooth barrel length of over 100 meters, along which a finned casing 97 kg would be accelerated by numerous small detonations at low pressure by branched charges along the barrel, each electrically fired in sequence.

The gun was still in its prototype stages, but Hitler was an enthusiastic supporter of the idea and ordered the maximum support to its development and its distribution. In August 1943 approved the construction of a gun battery HDP in France to complete the levels V1 and V2 missiles at London and the South East of England.

To reach England, the necessary length of the barrels of the weapons was equal to 127 meters, so you do not have to be moved and would have to be laid in a fixed site. A study conducted in early 1943 showed that the optimum location for its construction would have been in a hill with a rocky core in which the inclined drifts could be channeled to support the reeds. The site was identified by a fortification expert, Major Bock of Festungs-Pionier-Stab 27 of the Fifteenth Army based in the Dieppe area; it was a limestone hill near the village of Mimoyecques, 158 meters high and 165 km from London, which was then chosen to host the cannon. The hill where the facility was built was of lime with very little soil cover, and the layer of lime stretched several hundred meters below the surface, providing a deeper level rock but easy to dig. The lime is easy to dig and strong enough to dig tunnels without the use of wooden supports. Although the rail links for the site were poor, only a couple of kilometers were built west of the main railway line between Calais and Boulogne-sur-Mer Beach. Construction began in September 1943 with the construction of railway lines to support the work, while the excavation of the cannon wells began in October. The initial configuration included two to about 1,000 meters away parallel complexes, each with five drifts which were to contain a group of five tubes for the HDP cannon, for a total of 25 guns. The smooth bore design HDP allowed a much higher rate than was possible with conventional fire cannons. The entire battery would be capable of firing up to 10 rounds per minute, in theory capable of hitting London with 600 bullets per hour. Both structures had to be served by an underground railway tunnel connected to the main line Calais-Boulogne, while the storage underground tunnels for ammunition were dug to a depth of about 33 meters. The western site was abandoned at an early stage after being interrupted by Allied bombing, and only the eastern complex was built. The railway tunnel running in a straight line for a distance of about 630 meters. Along the west side there was an unloading platform which gave access to ten transverse galleries, numbered 3-13 by the Germans, placed perpendicular to the main tunnel at 24 meters intervals. On the east side of the tunnel it was arranged rooms intended to be used as warehouses, offices and accommodation for the garrison. The trains would enter the facility to download various materials and fuel for weapons. The galleries 6-10, the central group, gave access to guns, while the galleries 3-5 and 11-13 were intended to be used as access tunnels and perhaps also as storage areas. They were all connected by tunnel No. 2, which ran parallel to the main rail tunnel at a distance of 100 meters. The 6-10 galleries were instead connected by a second passage, designated gallery No. 1, parallel to the main tunnel at a distance of 24.5 meters. Further work there at different depths: 62 meters, 47 meters and 30 meters, each with different purposes:

- At 62 meters were dug to facilitate the removal of waste.
- Those 47 meters were destined to the treatment of exhaust gases from the guns.
- Those 30 meters gave access to the breeches of the guns.
- The lowest levels of functioning were accessible by elevator and mining cabins rooms.

The construction works were carried out by more than 5,000 workers, engineers mostly Germans borrowed from several companies including Mannesmann, Gute Hoffnungshütte, Krupp and Vereinigte Stahlwerke, with the addition of 430 miners recruited from the Ruhr and prisoners of war Soviets who were used as laborers. The intense bombing campaign of the Allies caused delays, but the construction work still continued at a high rate; the original plans had envisaged that the first battery of five guns to be ready by March 1944 and the full set of 25 cannons on 1 October 1944, but these deadlines were not met.

21 cm K 12 (E)

Certainly not comparable with V-3 21 cm Kanone 12 (Eisenbahnlafette), shortened to 21 cm K 12 (E), 21 cm model 12 caliber cannon on gun carriage rail, was a German railway gun used during World War II. The German company Krupp, during the period of the Weimar Republic, he continued theoretical research for a gun that would replace the Paris Gun, but it was with the rise to power of the Nazi Party who came to the funds for the trials, aimed at solving some of the problems more. The extremely high speed developed by the Paris Gun to reach the stratosphere, necessary for long-range, causing high consumption of the barrel, such that they should be used to project progressively larger diameter. Nevertheless, the useful life of the pipes was limited to just 50 shots. In addition, the explosion of a barrel was probably caused by the load in the wrong order for one of these bullets.

Krupp decided to use a scoring just 8 rows and milling of the corresponding grooves on the shell of the projectiles; is obviated so the need to arm the projectile of a massive copper forcing crown to impart rotation, which was a major cause of excessive wear of the pipes in the soul cannon of Paris. The sealing of the gases was ensured by a copper band with an asbestos and graphite gasket. In 1935 they were produced with these devices different test rods, known as 10.5 cm K 12 M, with its projectiles; compared with rods with conventional scoring (10.5 cm K 12 calls MKU), they showed that the idea of Krupp was correct. The K 12 (E) was mounted on a gun carriage to the beam, in turn mounted on two beam sottoaffusti, each of which resting on two bogies 5-axis, for a total of 20 axes for complex.

The barrel was mounted on a sleeve cradle with a hydropneumatic recoil system; two other shooting brake hydropneumatic connettevano the gun carriage to under carriages, allowing the entire gun-carriage of 98 cm recoil.

For transport the barrel was disconnected from the cradle firing brake and rearward of about 1.5 meters to reduce the overall length of the implant and bring it back within the gauge. The considerable length of the rod required external reinforcement to prevent that would bend under its own weight. Mumps were placed in far forward as possible to balance the barrel and reduce the strain on the hydraulic elevation presses; This posed the breech dangerously close to the terrain and the two sottoaffusti were then fitted with a hydraulic lifting system which increased by one meter distance between gun carriage and land. However at this location it was not possible to load the weapon and after each shot the gun carriage had to be lowered.

The rotation of the cradle on gun carriage was limited to 25 ', sufficient for precision pointing. For the gross K 12 (E) he could move on a curved section of track, or it could be loaded on a turntable Vögele or finally shoot his Special shooting rail. The turntable Vögele was constituted by a circular guide around a rotating pin, supporting a turntable on which the rail gun carriage was loaded thanks to a ramp; the platform was equipped at the ends of rollers that rested on the external guide. The special track was constituted by a prefabricated binary T-shaped, transported in the rail convoy of the cannon and put posing by a special crane wagon; at the intersection of the rod and cutting the two T trucks and front sottoaffusto were raised, turned 90 ° and resting on the rail cross-section; the two carriages moved along this thanks to electric motors, so brandeggiando the barrel; once in the tappet, the complex was locked to the rails. The first weapon was completed in 1938 and delivered to the German Army in March 1939; the weapon was a success, although the military did not welcome the need to raise and lower the gun carriage with each stroke. Trying to solve this problem on the second specimen, Krupp discovered that hydraulic elevation presses could work in weights and pressures higher than believed. The gun tube was thus redesigned pulling back the mumps. The second specimen was amended called K 12 N (E), while the first unit was thereafter referred to as K 12 V (E).

The two K 12 were assigned to the Eisenbahn-Artillerie-Batterie 701 (701ª railway artillery battery), stationed along the coast of the English Channel. In 1940, a bullet fired by a 12 K was found by the British authorities in the marshes of Rainham (Kent), 88.5 km away from the coast of occupied France. Overall, throughout the war the batteries 701 (E) fired 83 shots. The actual value of these weapons was still doubt the enormous size made them vulnerable to air attack; Moreover, not being able slewing independently, requiring the construction of infrastructure, platforms and tracks ad hoc.

www.ingramcontent.com/pod-product-compliance
Lightning Source LLC
Chambersburg PA
CBHW061747020426
42331CB00006B/1386